POTENTIALS
GUIDES FOR PRODUCTIVE LIVING

Wayne E. Oates, General Editor

YOUR FREEDOM TO BE WHOLE

by

HENLEE BARNETTE

THE WESTMINSTER PRESS
Philadelphia

Scripture quotations from the Revised Standard Version of the Bible are copyrighted 1946, 1952, © 1971, 1973 by the Division of Christian Education of the National Council of the Churches of Christ in the U.S.A. and are used by permission.

Scripture quotations from *The New English Bible* are copyright © The Delegates of the Oxford University Press and the Syndics of the Cambridge University Press, 1961, 1970, and are used by permission.

Book design by Alice Derr

First edition

Published by The Westminster Press ®
Philadelphia, Pennsylvania

PRINTED IN THE UNITED STATES OF AMERICA
2 4 6 8 9 7 5 3 1

Library of Congress Cataloging in Publication Data

Barnette, Henlee H.
  Your freedom to be whole.

  (Potentials)
  Bibliography: p.
  1. Christian life—Baptist authors. 2. Consolation.
I. Title II. Series.
BV4501.2.B3829 1984   248.4'86132   84-2381
ISBN 0-664-24526-9 (pbk.)

Affectionately dedicated to
Mazo
Loomis
Bill
Evelyn
Colleen
Roy

And to the memory of our sister
Nancy Dawn

Contents

Foreword		9
Acknowledgments		13
Prologue		15
1.	"I Want to Be Free"	17
2.	"I Am So Lonely"	33
3.	"I'm Bored to Death"	46
4.	"I Am So Anxious"	63
5.	"I Don't Trust Like I Did"	82
6.	"Is My Life Over?"	99
	Questions for Thought and Discussion	115
	Bibliography	117

Foreword

The eleven books in this series, Potentials: Guides for Productive Living, speak to your condition and mine in the life we have to live today. The books are designed to ferret out the potentials you have with which to rise above rampant social and psychological problems faced by large numbers of individuals and groups. The purpose of rising above the problems is portrayed as far more than merely your own survival, merely coping, and merely "succeeding" while others fail. These books with one voice encourage you to save your own life by living with commitment to Jesus Christ, and to be a creative servant of the common good as well as your own good.

In this sense, the books are handbooks of ministry with a new emphasis: coupling your own well-being with the well-being of your neighbor. You use the tools of comfort wherewith God comforts you to be a source of strength to those around you. A conscious effort has been made by each author to keep these two dimensions of the second great commandment of our Lord Jesus Christ in harmony with each other.

The two great commandments are summarized in Luke 10:25–28: "And behold, a lawyer stood up to put him to the test, saying, 'Teacher, what shall I do to inherit eternal life?' He said to him, 'What is written in the law? How do you

read?' And he answered, 'You shall love the Lord your God
with all your heart, and with all your soul, and with all your
strength, and with all your mind; and your neighbor as yourself.' And he said to him, 'You have answered right; do this,
and you will live.' "

Underneath the two dimensions of neighbor and self there
is also a persistent theme: The only way you can receive such
harmony of thought and action is by the intentional re-centering of your life on the sovereignty of God and the rapid
rejection of all idols that would enslave you. The theme,
then, of this series of books is that these words of Jesus are
the master guides both to the realization of your own potentials and to productive living in the nitty-gritty of your
day's work.

The books in this series are unique, and each claims your
attention separately in several ways.

First, these books address great social issues of our day,
but they do so in terms of your own personal involvement
in and responses to the problems. For example, the general
problem of the public school system, the waste in American
consumerism, the health hazards in a lack of rest and voca-
tional burnout, the crippling effects of a defective mental
outlook, and the incursion of Eastern mystical traditions into
Western Christian activism are all larger-then-life issues. Yet
each author translates the problem into the terms of day-to-
day living and gives concrete guidelines as to what you can
do about the problem.

Second, these books address the undercurrent of helplessness that overwhelming epidemic problems produce in you.
The authors visualize you throwing up your hands and saying: "There is nothing *anyone* can do about it." Then they
show you that this is not so, and that there are things *you* can
do about it.

Third, the authors have all disciplined themselves to stay
off their own soapboxes and to limit oratory about how awful the world is. They refuse to stop at gloomy diagnoses of

incurable conditions. They go on to deal with your potentials for changing yourself and your world in very specific ways. They do not let you, the reader, off the hook with vague, global utterances and generalized sermons. They energize you with a sense of hope that is generated by basic information, clear decision-making, and new directions taken by you yourself.

Fourth, these books get their basic interpretations and recommendations from a careful plumbing of the depths of the power of faith in God through Jesus Christ. They are not books that leave you with the illusion that you can lift yourself and your world by pulling hard at your own bootstraps. They energize and inspire you through the hope and strength that God in Christ is making available to you through the wisdom of the Bible and the presence of the living Christ in your life. Not even this, though, is presented in a namby-pamby or trite way. You will be surprised with joy at the freshness of the applications of biblical truths which you have looked at so often that you no longer notice their meaning. You will do many "double takes" with reference to your Bible as you read these books. You will find that the Bread of Life is not too holy or too good for human nature's daily food.

In this volume, Henlee Barnette, my colleague as Clinical Professor of Psychiatry and Behavioral Sciences in the University of Louisville School of Medicine, has brought his understanding as a Christian ethicist and pastoral counselor to bear on both the broad social issues and the intimately personal dilemmas involved in six major human emotions that shatter wholeness of heart and hinder productive living. No one who lives very long is exempt from these six emotions. They are testing experiences common to humankind. Do not be discouraged if you find yourself reflected on many pages. Simply read on, and you will find the author giving clear guidance about productive ways to make these emotions serve you rather than do you a disservice.

These feelings are both universally human and intensely personal. With a unique perspective on both dimensions, Barnette uses parable, metaphor, and personal witness to describe how these emotions feel and how they can fuel and energize your potentials rather than frustrate and erode your total well-being. His central concern is for wholeness of life, and he explains how you and I can "get it all together" in situations that tend to leave us in pieces of our best selves. Out of his own life and thought, which I know to have been a story of rising above adversity, Henlee Barnette brings the winnowed wisdom of years of courageous actualizing of potentials in his own life. You will read him with great benefit.

WAYNE E. OATES

Louisville, Kentucky

Acknowledgments

Because many individuals contribute to the publication of a book, I cannot acknowledge all those who had some input into the production of even this small volume. It is imperative, however, that I recognize those who made the greatest contributions. First, I owe much to my wife, Helen, who for a quarter of a century has shared significantly in my writing projects. This volume is no exception, for she suggested needed stylistic improvement.

Second, I am particularly indebted to Wayne E. Oates, my steadfast friend for forty-five years. He read the entire manuscript and made positive recommendations toward keeping the material focused on my readership.

Also I am grateful to my daughter, Martha Ann, staff writer for *The Louisville Times*, who read parts of the manuscript and helped to clarify some of the more murky statements and to hold in check my homiletical tendencies.

Finally, I am indebted to Judy Haas, who typed the rough draft, and to Tish Gardner, Eileen Long, Pattie McCollum, Connie Easterling, and Lisa Gennoe, secretaries at the Southern Baptist Theological Seminary, for typing the final copy of the manuscript.

H.B.

Louisville, Kentucky

Prologue

" . . . to let the broken victims go free"
(Luke 4:18, NEB)

Jesus saw in the prophetic statements of Isaiah (61:1–2 and 58:6) a summary of his own mission and message. One of his tasks was to set at liberty those who are "oppressed" or "bruised" (Luke 4:18). The New English Bible has the most accurate translation; Jesus was sent "to let the broken victims go free." The image is that of shattered pottery. We are indeed earthen vessels that suffer brokenness. To free those who are broken or shattered is part of the task that Jesus transferred to his disciples (John 20:21). The original statement by the ancient prophet referred primarily to those broken by political and social forces, but Jesus extends its meaning to include those broken psychologically and spiritually. He commits himself to setting you and me free to be whole.

The purpose of this small volume is to hold out hope for persons bruised or broken by oppression, a loss of personal control, or dehumanizing forces in society. You can be free *from* your feeling of brokenness. You can be free *to* be whole. Out of any shattering anxiety, loneliness, boredom, unforgiveness, distrust, or hopelessness you can be restored to the wholeness and integrity of being for which God created you and Christ died for you. Through the case studies and personal experiences recounted here, you can discover—and God will reveal to you—ways that your own broken life may be restored to wholeness and a genuine sense of well-being.

Chapter 1

"I Want to Be Free"

"I want to be free!" These were the words of a young man who came to my office back in the 1960s. He told me he wanted to be free from his parents' control, from the usual courses required for a college degree, from having to earn a living, and from the moral and social restraints of established society; he wanted to be free to do as he pleased. This young fellow was expressing a prevailing spirit of the time. Brought up in a family that shared responsibility and followed a strict code of conduct, he wanted to be able to shake off all restraints and be like others of his age.

People fall apart when their freedom of decision and action is taken from them or when they *think* that this has happened. If you feel trapped in a set of circumstances to which you see no end, in a noisome habit such as overeating, overdrinking, or overworking, in a marriage that you can't make work, or in a job that to you is impossible, you may often go to pieces. Even if you maintain a serene exterior, inside your private being you may feel fragmented, torn, and shattered. You yearn for wholeness. You seek the freedom to be whole. In this chapter, let's discuss your need to be free, to be whole. This need is basic to all the other issues in the succeeding chapters. Let's face it together.

Everyone Wants to Be Free

Inside you and me are both the desire and the drive to be free. Even the individual who chooses suicide is expressing a wish to be free—free from an unbearable life situation. Centuries ago the Jews at Masada chose mass suicide to avoid being slaves to the invading Romans.

The longing to be free is, in our culture, expressed in many ways. The United States was founded by patriots who wanted to be free of colonial control. In the Declaration of Independence, the thirteen states called themselves "free and independent states . . . absolved from all allegiance to the British crown." The yearning for freedom was expressed by the slaves of the Southern plantations as they sang spirituals with coded messages like "Didn't My Lord Deliver Daniel?" and "Follow the Drinking Gourd." (The drinking gourd was the Big Dipper constellation, which pointed to the North Star and helped to guide escaping slaves north.) Current popular songs reflect the desire for freedom from various restraints.

Not only lyrics but actions by individuals and groups show how cherished the goal of freedom is. The boat people from Vietnam and Cuba risked their lives on hazardous journeys to get into free America. Engraved on the Statue of Liberty is the message, "Give me . . . your huddled masses yearning to breathe free." That is the yearning of millions living in countries where basic freedoms are denied by dictatorial governments.

Sometimes freedom is cheapened by overfamiliarity with the words "freedom" and "free" as used in television and other advertising. Among the expressions heard are "caffeine free, sugar free, odor free, toll free, free of embarrassment, free of insects." Sometimes we ask our friends, "Are you free this evening?"

But *real* freedom for most American citizens means having privileges that we would not trade for any other citizenship. A quarter of a century ago I spent several weeks in Russia and some Russian-controlled countries. Our delegation studied problems in the Soviet Union, and our stay was climaxed by a two-hour conference with Premier Nikita Khrushchev in his office in the Kremlin. At all times I and my fellow group members felt that we were not free, that we were being watched constantly. When, at the end of our trip, we sailed into New York Harbor, I was so elated I snapped eight pictures of the Statue of Liberty! I felt like the serviceman returning from Europe at the end of World War I who exclaimed as he saw the statue, "Old Lady, if you ever see me again, you will have to turn around!"

What It Means to Be Free

Some argue that we really do not have any freedom, that the course of our lives is already determined for us by some outside power or fate. But I maintain that, for all practical purposes, we do have a measure of freedom. We are not merely puppets on strings manipulated by a divine super-puppeteer. I wonder if you've heard the story about Lyman Beecher, a noted New England preacher of the nineteenth century. In his day there was a heated debate about "predestination," the belief that all one's life is determined by God and that people really have no freedom of choice.

> One weekend he was to exchange pulpits with a neighboring minister who held to a rigid view of predestination, but Beecher was a liberal on that point. On Sunday morning each started out going to the other church, and met midway. As they paused, the neighboring minister said: "Doctor Beecher, I wish to call to your attention that before the creation of the world God arranged that you were to preach in my pulpit and I in yours on this particular Sabbath." "Is that so?" said Beech-

er, glaring at him. "Then I won't do it!" And turning his horse around, he returned to his church.
(Harry Emerson Fosdick, *On Being a Real Person*,
p. 15; Harper & Brothers, 1943)

Freedom is easier to picture, illustrate, and feel personally
than it is to define. It means different things to different
people. For example, on the day I am writing these words,
the news has come that the evangelical Christians who took
refuge for nearly five years in the basement of the American
Embassy in Moscow have been allowed to leave the Soviet
Union. Surely their concept of freedom is quite different
from that of the youth I mentioned at the beginning of this
chapter.

There are several kinds of freedom: personal, social, political, and intellectual. Freedom is so all-inclusive that the
ordinary dictionary presents about a dozen ideas that are part
of freedom. Also, freedom is usually related to liberty. The
words "freedom" and "liberty" are often used interchange-
ably. Freedom more often refers to the absence of restraint
or repression. On the other hand, liberty commonly implies
that previous restraints have been removed. For example, the
liberty to speak at a political meeting is a freedom restored.

Freedom is like a flame that burns within us. Although we
feel its warmth, words fail us when we try to define it. We
all yearn for it because it is a basic human desire. Real freedom finally forces us to choose and be responsible for our
decisions. This is why freedom can be so frightening. It is
also feared by both religious and secular organizations, for it
is seen as a threat to privileged power. Independent freedom is often seen as an enemy by some of those wanting control and power.

Yes, freedom can be frightening. According to Berdyaev,
the Russian Christian philosopher, "the mass of mankind has
no love for freedom, and is afraid of it" (*The Beginning and
the End*, p. 215; London: Geoffrey Bles, 1952). He is right

in saying that people are afraid of freedom and wrong when he declares that they do not love it. Many people love freedom but lack the courage to take on the responsibility or to pay the price true freedom requires.

Obviously, in one small volume we cannot deal thoroughly with the many facets of freedom. So I shall focus here on your personal freedom. Its relation to your spiritual and psychological being will receive the most emphasis. Being related to the truth as it is in Jesus (Eph. 4:23), freedom has both personal and social meaning. The apostle John states, "If you continue in my word, you are truly my disciples, and you will know the truth, and the truth will make you free. . . . So if the Son makes you free, you will be free indeed" (John 8:32, 36).

Your Freedom and Other Values

Freedom is false if it is not related to other virtues and values. Your Christian freedom is related to the truth as it is in Jesus. This is more than the kind of truth one is supposed to provide under oath in the courtroom or the kind known as scientifically proven fact. Rather, it is truth as expressed in the person of Jesus Christ as Lord of life. Jesus is the way, the truth, and the life (John 14:6). To follow Christ is to follow the truth; to reject him is to miss the truth and the road to life as he wants us to have it.

As Thomas à Kempis wrote:

> Without the way
>   there is no going;
> Without the truth
>   there is no knowing;
> Without the life
>   there is no living.
> (*The Imitation of Christ,*
> III, 66)

Freedom is related to responsibility. You are responsible for your own decisions, for your own actions—for your successes and failures. Do you seek to avoid responsibility by shifting it to others, by passing the buck? You probably remember the classic example of this from the story of Moses and his brother Aaron. While Moses was up on Mt. Sinai communing with God, Aaron was keeping the Israelites (who had recently escaped from Egypt and Pharaoh's control) in line until his brother returned. The mass of exiles became restless (perhaps a bit bored?) and persuaded Aaron to let them forge a spectacular golden calf to worship. Moses was furious when he descended from the mountain with the stone tablets of the Ten Commandments. After venting his rage on the idol, he angrily demanded an explanation of Aaron. In what has to be one of the best examples of passing the buck (in this case, a calf), Aaron replied that the people had been mean and upset and wanted something to worship, so he instructed them to bring him any gold they had. Then, with a look of disarming innocence, Aaron told his brother, "I cast it [the gold] into the fire, and [wonder of wonders] out came this calf" (Ex. 32:24). We are not told what Moses' reply to that alibi was.

Centuries later, Pilate tried to shift the responsibility for the condemnation of Jesus, and he dramatized this by washing his hands. But shifting the blame by either clever words or crafty action cannot free us from our own unique responsibility.

Freedom from What?

Freedom has two sides: freedom *from* and freedom *to* (or *for*). In the Bible, different aspects of freedom are stressed. The exodus story stresses freedom from the political power of the Egyptians over the Israelites. John's Gospel is concerned with freedom from the world. And the letters of Paul have much to say about freedom from the law. But all speak of freedom to serve the one God and Father of our Lord.

Specifically, what do you need to be freed from in order that your life may be fuller and more productive?

Freedom from Self-Centeredness

The first thing you need is freedom from self and self-centeredness. In psychiatry, radical self-centeredness is called the narcissistic personality disorder (you will recall that Narcissus was the mythological youth who fell in love with his own reflection). In theology, it is called sin.

When you are egocentric or self-centered, you are thinking that everyone else's thoughts and actions must surely be directed toward you. They, in their own self-centeredness, are more likely to think that your thoughts are directed toward them! Some people have built huge barriers or walls around themselves and have real difficulty in admitting that the world does not center on them, their wishes, and their actions. It is difficult for others to reach across those barriers and relate meaningfully to them.

Not only do self-centered people try to control the manner in which others relate to them, they try to bring God into their own control of reality. Self-centeredness is definitely not God-centeredness.

How do we get deliverance from the sin of self-centeredness? It is an ongoing struggle for the Christian; but it is rooted in sincere, honest confession of being other than God-centered (that is, of being sinful) and in commitment to God in Christ as Lord of our life. This can be a continual experience; it begins with a realization and an admission of our own need for this kind of re-centering of our life. It may be felt in a sense of guilt that comes as a result of much Bible study and prayer. It may result from the consistent example set by another person's life. Or it may occur when we least expect it. That's how it happened to me over half a century ago. Let me tell you about it.

At age nineteen I was a school dropout who had never
seen the inside of a high school. I had already worked for six
long years in a cotton mill near my home in the South. Such
work is hard and repetitive—but it makes you tough. And I
was that; my whole family was. We were transplanted mountain folks who had reluctantly left the poverty of our Sugar
Loaf Mountain cabin to live in a company mill house in order to survive.

Other neighbors in the mill houses knew hardship and
hard work too. The man next door, who had quit school after the fourth grade, worked as a mill weaver. He was a de-
vout Christian. One day he came over to our house to invite
me to go with him to a revival meeting the next night at one
of the small "mill hill" churches. I resented this man's invading my privacy; I also felt embarrassed and uncomfortable
when he was talking about religion. That was something we
tough guys spoke about only by making fun of it. This man
was serious! To get rid of him in a hurry, I promised to go
with him, knowing all the while that I was planning to be in
the next county at that time anyway. But he was right there
at my house the next night before I could sneak away.

Reluctantly, I said I'd keep my promise to go with him but
insisted we first go by "the shacks," a cluster of small cafés
and a pool hall on the edge of town where toughies hung out.
I wanted to have at least one of my own kind along. After
some lengthy persuasion, Red Holmes agreed to help me out
by accompanying us.

Quietly we entered the small wooden frame church and sat
on the back pew made of planks. Rev. Wade H. James was
already into his sermon. (He had only an eighth-grade education, but I discovered later that he was a very wise man.)
His subject was "The Great Physician" and the text was from
Jeremiah: "Is there no balm in Gilead? Is there no physician
there?" (Jer. 8:22). Somehow his words seemed directed
straight at me.

As he preached in his simple but straightforward style, I

was able through the words he used to connect what he was saying with the condition I knew, in truth, my own soul to be in. It was as if an electric cord had finally been plugged into an empty socket so that the power of the Holy Spirit could be carried through to me. I felt the impact of Brother James's words, and I felt keenly my need to re-center my life.

When, at the end of his sermon, the call was given for those who wished to do so to come to the front and make a commitment to Christ, I slipped out into the narrow aisle, went forward with my head bowed, and took a seat on the mourners' bench. There I prayed to God in simple but heart-felt words, "Here is my life, Lord. Take it for your own glory." For me in that moment, the bondage of sin was broken. I felt as clean inside as if I had been washed with a miracle soap. I felt cleansed, new, free, whole.

When I looked farther down the mourners' bench, I saw my father. He had come forward to make his own commitment, yet neither of us had been aware the other was there! We embraced in tearful joy.

Meanwhile my buddy, Red Holmes, had bolted out the back door when the altar call was given. It was the parting of the ways for us. I never saw Red again but learned later that he had been jailed for murder. It had indeed been a time of decision for each of us.

Freedom from Guilt

Guilt is a complex feeling. It gets all mixed up with anxiety, fear, pain, remorse, shame, depression, and the violation of the standards of society. But you know that you can sort out this mixture with a little rest and a lot of prayer. You know what real guilt is, for there have been times when the degree of your guilt was equal to the act committed. For example, I talked with a man dying of lung cancer. For years his physician had warned him against smoking, especially after surgery. But the patient kept on smoking. Now he felt guilty about what he had done to himself, his wife, and his five children, for he was leaving them to pay his debts. His guilt was real. He knew what real guilt is.

On the other hand, you may not be so well acquainted with psychotic, unreal guilt feelings. One patient confessed to his doctor that he had recently caused a large destructive blast in their local area. The doctor reminded the man that he had been a patient in the hospital at the time of the blast and could not possibly have caused it. The patient felt so keenly the anguish suffered by those whose homes were damaged that he felt he must bear the guilt for it too. Another compulsive patient was troubled by the "Lady Macbeth syndrome"; she engaged in obsessive handwashing. She would keep objects in her house spotlessly clean too. But one day she showed up at our hospital with hands literally scrubbed raw. She had "washed" her hands in lye. And a grossly overweight man confided, "I eat because I feel guilty. I can concentrate on food and forget all I've done."

Therapists and psychiatrists and specially trained pastors may help such patients in dealing with neurotic and psychotic guilt. But for everyday garden-variety sin there is one effective therapy: a sense of forgiveness for hurting others or violating the laws of God.

Confession to God can bring you forgiveness of sin if you can forgive yourself. Confession can be glib and meaningless. But yours won't be. Yours will include contrition (sorrow for your sin) and restitution (setting right those things that can be set right without destroying others). You can confess directly to God or to another person who believes in the priesthood of all believers; that is, that each believer has free access to God. This is the "spiritual ministry" of every Christian—to point all who are burdened with guilt to God, who forgives and reconciles you to yourself, to others, and to Christ, who takes away the sin of the world.

In the Old Testament story, King David committed adultery with his neighbor's wife and arranged to have her husband killed. Then David had a visit from the prophet Nathan.

> And the LORD sent Nathan to David. He came to him, and said to him, "There were two men in a certain city, the one rich and the other poor. The rich man had very many flocks and herds; but the poor man had nothing but one little ewe lamb, which he had bought. And he brought it up, and it grew up with him and with his children; it used to eat of his morsel, and drink from his cup, and lie in his bosom, and it was like a daughter to him. Now there came a traveler to the rich man, and he was unwilling to take one of his own flock or herd to prepare for the wayfarer who had come to him, but he took the poor man's lamb, and prepared it for the man who had come to him." Then David's anger was greatly kindled against the man; and he said to Nathan, "As the LORD lives, the man who has done this deserves to die; and he shall restore the lamb fourfold, because he did this thing, and because he had no pity." (II Sam. 12:1–7)

One can see David's face flaming with anger when he heard of the injustice done to the poor man. At this point Nathan did some direct counseling. Looking the king straight in the eye, he said, "*You* are the man." And he focused on David's wickedness. Obviously the king got the message, for he declared, "I have sinned against the LORD." Psalm 51 is attributed to David. It contains those elements necessary for the erasing of guilt: sorrow for sin, confession, turning from sin, forgiveness, reconciliation, rejoicing, and a readiness to reach out and help others broken by sin.

Freedom from Fear

President Franklin Roosevelt once declared that "the only thing we have to fear is fear itself." But there are other things that frighten us, things that can throw us into near panic: loud or sudden noises, being in closed-in places, being in high places, being stranded in unfamiliar places, driving across high bridges, being in crowds. There are the fears of having committed the unpardonable sin, of being made to appear foolish, of being tested, of thunderstorms and lightning.

One woman who does not seem bothered by thunderstorms and who actually believes a lightning display to be a thing of spectacular beauty says that as a child she was taught to repeat the following verse whenever she was frightened:

> The thunder rolls,
>   the rain dashes;
> The wind blows,
>   the lightning flashes;
> But I will not fear—
> God will take care of me.

On the other hand, I once knew a farmer who had an irrational fear of storms. Even if he was in the field working, when dark clouds approached he would race to the house, calling his wife and two small children; they would all go to the bedroom and hide in the bed with the covers pulled over them until the thunderstorm passed.

Millions of people are trapped in the prison of fear. You can break out of this prison if you do the following things: First, face up to your fears. This is the first step in coping with them. For example, if your greatest fear is storms, study them as a hobby; learn all you can about hurricanes and tornadoes. If your fear is dependency in old age, begin to plan for that period of your life. If you are afraid of death, try to see that it is a part of the totality of life. If your fear is "phobic" or "excessive," you can get professional help. (In Virginia, there are policemen whose major duty is to help panicked drivers get across the $5^1/_2$-mile-long Chesapeake Bay Bridge!)

Fear can be destructive to personality. Through faith in

Christ, fear can be conquered. John Newton knew this when
he wrote:

> How sweet the name of Jesus sounds
> In a believer's ear!
> It soothes his sorrows, heals his wounds,
> And drives away his fear.

Freedom from Prejudice

Maybe you are trapped in the prison of prejudice against
particular ethnic or racial minorities. Such prejudice is destructive to your life and can leave you spiritually and
psychologically broken. Prejudice is the false notion that
some races of people are inherently inferior to others. This
widespread myth is frequently behind the denial of funda-
mental human rights and sometimes even causes war.

I have found it helpful in combating prejudice in my own
life to look to Jesus and some of his followers as models. Jesus, of course, taught that you are to love your neighbor, including your enemy (Matt. 5:44–48; cf. Matt. 22:36–40). Peter discovered that "God shows no partiality" (Acts 10:34).
Paul declared that in the light of the resurrection of Christ
we are to "regard no one from a human point of view" (II
Cor. 5:16). Paul also declared, "There is neither Jew nor
Greek, there is neither slave nor free, there is neither male
nor female; for you are all one in Christ Jesus" (Gal. 3:28).
That is to say, there is no place for discrimination based on
race, class, or sex.

I also find courage when I think of a later Paul, one of my
students at Southern Baptist Theological Seminary. On De-
cember 4, 1956, Rev. Paul Turner, pastor of the First Baptist Church of Clinton, Tennessee, escorted a group of black
children from their homes into the public school, which—to
the outrage of many citizens in the small community—had
been ordered desegregated by the court. Tensions were high
that brisk morning as the young pastor emerged from the

school and made his way through the jeering, taunting heck-
lers to go to his church. Then several burly men cornered
Paul and beat him with their fists. As one eyewitness re-
marked, "That preacher put up a good fight." But he carried
a facial scar from that brutal attack until the day he died many
years later.

Paul Turner's act of courage and his suffering for what he
felt was right seemed to bring into focus for the towns-
people the way their community was being torn apart. The
slow healing process that did take place seems to have grown
out of that event. The happenings at Clinton were depicted
and analyzed on national television by Edward R. Murrow,
and I am convinced they caused other citizens to look deep
within their own souls to ask, "Could I ever be a part of that
kind of attack?" or "Could I care that much about doing what
is right?"

Other role models for me have been two elderly gentle-
men: Dr. W. R. Cullom, who taught me Old Testament at
Wake Forest College, and S. L. Morgan, a distinguished
preacher of North Carolina. At the ripe ages of ninety-five
and ninety, they covenanted to study together in order to
free themselves of what they felt was culturally imposed
prejudice. They met regularly to study racial prejudice in a
scholarly fashion and to share insights about how to move beyond injustice and the denial of civil rights.

Freedom for What?

If our freedom is not *from* something negative and destructive or *to* something positive and creative, then it is a false
freedom, not a genuine one. The young man I mentioned at
the beginning of this chapter was seeking freedom from responsibility and to (or for) self-centered existence without
concern for others or the values of a religious faith. That
freedom would fail him eventually because it would be de- '
structive.

Genuine freedom frees you *for* something. It is freedom that enables you to be your best self, using your own unique gifts. It liberates you through the assurance of forgiveness, giving you confidence in the love and the re-centering of your life in Christ. It is freedom for wholehearted action and singleness of mind. It is freedom to be whole, to respond to life with integrity and unity of being.

Freedom to Love

Thus you are free to love. This is not the "free love" some irresponsible people want, but the love that wills the well-being of all God's creatures and creation. It involves love for your neighbor and also for God's good earth.

Love is the answer to an unstable and confused world. Bertrand Russell, a non-Christian and a philosopher of note, believed that love was the answer. In a lecture delivered at Columbia University, he stated that it was not just any kind of love; it was "Christian love" that would hold the world on a more steady course (*The New York Times,* Nov. 16, 1950, p. 27). What the world needs is the power of love to enable us to see and react with each other and not against each other. Where love reigns there is freedom, peace, and justice, brotherly and sisterly care, solidarity, and stability.

Freedom to Hope

True freedom generates hope. It is the ethical seedbed of hope. To be free is to begin to hope. To live in hope is to anticipate, to expect. Hope can jump the boundaries or limits, scale the walls of imprisonment, and help the human spirit soar a little closer to God. Hope gives meaning to the confinement in which we sometimes find ourselves.

For example, I am reminded of my ninety-two-year-old father-in-law, who is now wheelchair-bound in a fine nursing home in Virginia. For over sixty years he was a Baptist preacher who ministered in several towns along U.S. Highway 11 in that state. When his daughter visited him recently at the nursing home, he confided that he did indeed need some items he didn't have.

"Do tell me what you need," she replied eagerly, "and I'll bring them next time I come."

Shifting his weight a bit in the wheelchair and fingering the collar of his bathrobe, the old pastor said with dignity, "I need some of my shirts with starched collars, Anne. Otherwise, when they call me to preach, I won't have any proper shirts to wear!"

In spite of the toll of many years, my father-in-law lives with the hope that he can continue to be made whole through the exercise of his calling to serve his Lord. The restraints that bind him to a wheelchair cannot shatter that hope or his spirit. He is bound by infirmities, yet free because he is whole.

Freedom is unifying your spirit in the freedom of Christ. *That* freedom is your gift of wholeness. You can claim it for your own.

Chapter 2

"I Am So Lonely"

Have you ever experienced the feeling of being terribly lonely? In this you may feel alone, but you have a large company of persons who feel as you do. Loneliness is another one of those bruising, shattering experiences of people to whom God in Christ came to bring the freedom to be whole. Recently I talked with a woman who kept repeating over and over again, "I am so lonely." She was a widow who had now also lost, through an untimely death, her only son. This woman felt that her son had been the one person she could really count on. Now that he was gone, her loneliness seemed unbearable.

"My weekends," she said, "are like rows and rows of tombstones."

Loneliness Everywhere

If you are like me, you have struggled with the feeling of loneliness for most of your life. It appears to be a basic part of being human and is considered by many to be one of the most common afflictions in American life. According to some medical doctors, loneliness can even bring on premature death. Yet it is seldom mentioned in most books on psychology, internal medicine, or psychiatry.

Have you noticed that loneliness is one of the most often

used themes in popular songs? Our children (and often adults too) spend millions of dollars every year on records and tapes with lyrics about loneliness, its causes and effects. Television commercials are filled with ideas about loneliness: ways to avoid it and ways to cope with it. In one such commercial, a lighthouse dweller rows to the mainland to pick up a washing machine repairman. Once at the lighthouse, the mechanic finds only the wire to a small plug in need of repair and says with irritation, "You could have fixed that yourself easy." "I know," replies the lighthouse keeper sheepishly, "but it gets mighty lonely out here!"

As Carl Sandburg observed:

> There are men and women so lonely
> they believe God, too, is lonely.
> (*The Complete Poems of Carl Sandburg,* rev. ed.,
> p. 293; Harcourt Brace Jovanovich, 1970)

Why has loneliness actually been neglected by the experts and specialists? One reason is that it is difficult to put into words, to understand, and to change. Then too, there is the wrongheaded belief that loneliness is a flaw of character, that it is a sign of weakness. Anyone, it is popularly believed, should be able to overcome loneliness. So masses of people seem not to regard it as a medical problem, a problem of health, a problem of wholeness. What is it like to be lonely, and in what ways does the good news of God in Christ put you and me back together again, making us whole and setting us free from the paralyzing bondage of loneliness?

What It's Like to Be Lonely

Loneliness is a distressful feeling that comes from being deprived of relationships to persons who make life meaningful. It can be caused by the loss of a job, a loved one, or even a membership in a particular organization, or by a profound change in life circumstances. A cluster of feelings may indicate loneliness. Among these are feelings of boredom, desperation, low self-esteem, and depression.

How do lonely people feel and what do they do? Some lonely people cry easily, sleep a lot, overeat, watch television endlessly, get drunk, or engage compulsively in frenzied amusements, shallow sex, or just shopping or telephoning friends. A good case could be made for "shoppingitis" and "telephonitis." Reasons for being lonely may be living alone, having no close friends, being shut in, finding yourself rejected or neglected by loved ones, or simply being a long way from home in a strange land and culture.

The last kind of loneliness became very real to me the summer I visited Russia. Our boat trip on the Volga River included a stop at a rather isolated spot. Eager to learn more about the country, I left the excursion boat for a closer look at the scenery, but when I returned to the dock, the boat was nowhere in sight. Now believe me! Sitting alone on a riverbank in a foreign country, particularly the Soviet Union, is about the loneliest thing I want ever to have happen to me. What a relief when another tourist boat finally came by and I was able to return to Moscow and to rejoin my group!

Another profoundly lonely feeling is that brought on by the loss of a long-cherished relationship. Recently I received a touching letter from one of the most intellectually stimulating professors I had years ago in college. He shared the depth of his loneliness as follows:

> The situation in this house during the last three years has been severe. My wife suffered a stroke and required hospitalization for seventeen months before her death. Just prior to her illness, I was hospitalized for seven weeks, and I am left with a crippled leg. Loneliness is now almost unbearable, being left alone after 57 years together.

Because of all the demands and pressures on their ability to adapt, students are often lonely people. Many times they are separated from family, support groups, and the familiar settings of home and are trying to forge new friendships. They can thus become prime targets for cults, both religious and secular. Recruiters from cults such as The Way, the Unification Church (the "Moonies"), and the Children of God can easily spot these lonely young people and "love bomb" them (show them a lot of affection, attention, and support) to lure them into cult membership.

Like students, those in military service can experience painful loneliness. After giving a lecture to a group at a large military base, I felt I had actually failed to connect with my audience. So after the session I sought to get insight from the chaplain about the major problem of these soldiers. When I questioned the chaplain, I felt his reply to my question would be something like "drugs, alcohol, going AWOL." But instead he answered without hesitation, "The biggest problem of the military personnel here is *loneliness!*"

This malaise is no respecter of persons. It can be found among all groups regardless of age, profession, class, or culture. Loneliness goes with being human.

Loneliness and Health

As has been indicated, loneliness is a condition that can be a health hazard. These feelings of despair, anxiety, and grief, of being unwanted and unloved, can lead to suicide or promote a slow suicide. Lynch and others have shown that reflected in our hearts is a biological basis for our need for loving human relationships (James J. Lynch, *The Broken Heart: The Medical Consequences of Loneliness*). He says that when we fail to fulfill this need, it can be dangerous. His research shows that for single persons, widows, and divorcees the statistical probability of experiencing premature death is 2 to 10 times higher than for individuals who live with others.

And what are the symptoms of loneliness? Lynch identifies them as depression, anxiety, migraine headaches, ulcers, and hypertension or high blood pressure (*U.S. News & World Report*, June 30, 1980, p. 48).

Of course, not every person living alone is endangering his or her health. So do not rush out to find a mate or a group with whom to live. Many people find living alone to be rewarding; they are content and healthy. But generally it is healthier to be living with someone. Just keeping a pet in your home may prolong your life. For one thing, you can talk to an animal and it won't dispute your word or nag you. Also, as you care for and pamper your pet, your own blood pressure will very likely be reduced. The interaction can be therapeutic.

Creative Uses of Loneliness

Jesus Christ sets you and me free of the paralyzing power of loneliness by the strength of his Spirit to change our angle of vision of what is happening to us. Loneliness can be something different from the darkness I have just described. It can be seen and felt as opportunity and not as oppression, as creative and not shattering, as wholesome, not devastating.

With all that negative discussion, it can be helpful to realize that loneliness can, in some cases, be used creatively by the lonely person. Like other life experiences, it has value and can be transformed. (See Clark E. Moustakas, *The Touch of Loneliness*.) Loneliness can be converted into creative solitude. The person who achieves beyond the level of most others in family living, literature, the sciences, art, and even politics tends often to feel lonely. That sort of productive life calls for discipline and a focus upon one aspect of your world. It puts you in a class by yourself. Similarly, scientists, inventors, and explorers are forced to isolate themselves in order to get their work done. Thus, some vocations involve withdrawing from others to realize a calling to accomplish an unheard-of thing, to minister to outcast persons, to think thoughts rarely considered—or even to sacrifice in order to enable someone you love to do these things.

Writing

Writing can be a therapy, a healing act. You can positively manage your loneliness by writing. You may want to try keeping a journal or a diary to cope with your own sense of loneliness. Remember that much literature which continues to be read centuries after it was written was born from loneliness that lonely people, by God's help, transformed into solitude. Some of the greatest books and essays in history were written in lonely jails. Paul the apostle wrote some of his letters behind prison walls. John Bunyan wrote *The Pilgrim's Progress* and Martin Luther King, Jr., wrote "Letter from a Birmingham Jail" from behind bars. Malcolm X was another writer who used his experiences in jail effectively.

Even children sometimes put their thoughts in writing, especially the lonely ones. An eighth-grader, a flutist, who felt quite alone after the breakup of her family, wrote recently:

> The sound of silence,
> That I cannot bear.
> So into empty spaces,
> I put my music there.
> When I play,
> The wind sways the trees,
> Dancing and whispering
> In my created breeze.
> Colors swirl.
> I'm floating out,
> The music is ringing;
> I'm free of the drought
> Of silence.

Writing is one therapy I have found to be personally healing and one that I suggest for lonely people whom I counsel. The writing may or may not be done for publication. I suggest it because sometimes we will put thoughts on paper when we are reluctant to speak them. Also, it gives an opportunity to read and reread the words with a bit more objectivity. It captures our thoughts in a moment of time as a camera catches a scene. It can help us "think on paper" and perhaps rearrange some patterns of thought or ideas.

The famous monk Thomas Merton wrote more than sixty books. Many of them were "thinking in print," since he lived out much of his life in solitude and silence. Indeed, his designated biographer, John Howard Griffin, said of Merton, "He literally meditated on paper. I have said that he could not scratch his nose without writing about it." (See "In Search of Thomas Merton," in *The Thomas Merton Studies Center,* p. 18; Santa Barbara: Unicorn Press, 1971.) Merton wrote:

> Man's loneliness, in fact, is the loneliness of God. That is why it is such a great thing for a man to discover his solitude and learn to live in it. For there he finds that he and God are one: that God is alone as he himself is alone. That God wills to be alone in man. (R. A. Cashen, *Solitude in the Thought of Thomas Merton,* p. 64; Kalamazoo: Cistercian Publications, 1981)

Transforming Loneliness Into Solitude

The loving grace of Christ quietly takes our loneliness—always with our permission—and transforms it into solitude. The fruits of solitude are the purifying process of the interior desert in which false ideas, illusions, and delusions are burned away. You then discover your real identity as a child of God. You gradually shift toward faith, hope, and the enrichment of love by compassion; you gain a new perspective on yourself, others, and the world. You begin to feel yourself being "pulled together" as you pray, for Christ's love holds you together and you sense a new wholeness and personal control (II Cor. 5:14).

God helps you to transform loneliness into solitude through his creation, nature. For brief times the sounds of birds, the whispering of trees, the majesty of the sky, the awesomeness of the ocean can refresh you; yet nature cannot answer the most bothersome questions of your lonely mind. You are compelled to the world of people for better answers, to people who can, without words, share your solitude in silence.

Another way to find solitude is in reading poetry, listening to music, and participating in art. But just about everything in our society tends to deprive you of your solitude. Even when you pray, you are tempted to make God a partner in conversation and use him as a way of escape from solitude.

But your greatness can arise from centering your attention on God within your inner being. When you are separated from the world, you are able to look at it, to transform it. Because you have a quiet, private, God-given center, you, when alone, are free.

Some Other Ways of Looking at Loneliness

Paul Tillich offers some thoughtful reflections on loneliness and solitude in *The Eternal Now* (Charles Scribner's Sons, 1963). He observes that a person is alone and is aware of this fact and wonders why. He or she seeks to overcome being alone. This sense of aloneness can be neither endured nor escaped.

"Loneliness can be conquered," claims Tillich, "only by those who can bear solitude" (p. 21). Since we all have a natural desire for solitude, we want to find it with joy and courage. Whitehead speaks of religion as "what the individual does with his own solitariness." If this is true, then each way we seek solitude is religious experience.

For Tillich, the word "loneliness" expresses the pain of being alone and the word "solitude" expresses the glory of being alone. He observes that people feel the pain of loneliness when those are gone who helped us to forget we were alone. Then there are those who are lonely even in crowds, those whose love is rejected, those who are lonely because of guilt, and those (all of us) who fear the loneliness of having to die.

Tillich concludes that you and I cannot become creative without solitude. "One hour of conscious solitude," he says, "will enrich your creativity far more than hours of trying to learn the creative process" (p. 23). He thinks that an hour of solitude may bring us closer to our loved ones than many hours of communication. "We can," he says, "take them with us to the hills of eternity" (p. 24).

Ways of Dealing Creatively with Loneliness

I recall one patient who had a lovely bouquet of flowers on the dresser in her room in the psychiatric ward. After I had expressed a word of admiration for its beauty, she asked me to look at the small attached card. It read: *From one who loves you very much.* I kidded her a bit about her boyfriend. Then she informed me that she had been in the hospital for days and no one had come to see her. So she ordered the flowers for herself!

In my own struggle to transform loneliness into solitude and creative social action, I do several things. Stimulating books help. Indeed, I am a bookaholic. My wife has already told the salespeople at the bookstores, "Don't let him have any more!"

Good music helps me reach a satisfactory state of solitude. My wife loves classical music. I do now, for she taught me its values. Listening to great music helps me transform aloneness into nourishing solitude.

I love nature; for me it is therapeutic. "The heavens declare the glory of God and the firmament showeth his handiwork," said the psalmist. But I must approach nature with reverence to see God and to enjoy solitude. Elizabeth Barrett Browning put it this way:

> Earth's crammed with heaven,
> And every common bush afire with God;
> But only he who sees, takes off his shoes,
> The rest sit round it and pluck blackberries.

Jesus Our Model

Jesus often withdrew from the crowds to be alone and to pray. "He went up on the mountain by himself to pray. When evening came, he was there alone" (Matt. 14:23). He moved from solitude to society in a rhythmic pattern. In solitude, he renewed his strength for the ministry of teaching, preaching, and healing.

If Jesus needed solitude, how much more do his disciples? Unfortunately, you and I may turn aside to pray, keep up a conversation with God as a partner, yet never reach the state of solitude. In solitude it is more important to listen to God than to tell him all your troubles, which he knows already. Let God transform your loneliness into solitude by a sense of his presence in the inner sanctuary of your heart. Only then will you and I be able to help others transform their loneliness into solitude and meaningful social action.

Loneliness and Listening for the Voice of the Almighty

You may hear the voice of God in your loneliest moments. Remember the experience of the Hebrew prophet Elijah. Jezebel, wife of Ahab the king of Israel, wanted to force her religion, the worship of the god Baal, upon the people of Israel. In a kind of contest, Elijah met the prophets of Baal. Each side challenged the other to prove which God was the true God. Sacrificial altars were built; the consensus was that the true God would respond with fire on the altar and the others would be judged impostors. Only the God of Israel answered by fire, and when that happened, Elijah had the prophets of Baal killed.

When Jezebel heard about this, she became enraged and threatened Elijah's life. He fled into the wilderness, going on to Horeb (Mt. Sinai), where much earlier in history God had given Moses the Ten Commandments. Alone and in great despair, Elijah hid in a cave. God asked him what he was doing there. Elijah said, "I have been very jealous for the LORD, the God of hosts; for the people of Israel have forsaken thy covenant, thrown down thy altars, and slain thy prophets with the sword; and I, even I only, am left; and they seek my life, to take it away" (I Kings 19:10). Then God reminded Elijah in his sense of loneliness that there were seven thousand in Israel who had not bowed to Baal. A whole community of his kind was out there, people among whom he could find fellowship and support. God also had new tasks for Elijah: to anoint kings and to appoint his own successor.

No longer feeling alone, and with a renewal of courage and a sense of God's presence with him, Elijah set about fulfilling the tasks God had set before him.

At the times of our greatest loneliness and fear, we too can hear that still, small voice of God through "the sound of silence."

Loneliness, Dreams, and Deeds

Loneliness may force you to think, brainstorm, even dream big. You can turn dreams into deeds sometimes. Clarence Jordan was one who did just that. Born in southern Georgia, he grew up seeing injustice in the way blacks were treated and vowed to do something about it. After receiving a degree in agriculture from the University of Georgia and a doctorate in New Testament Greek, he and his wife, Florence, established Koinonia Farm near Americus, Georgia (not far from Plains), in 1942.

Clarence's dream was to have a community made up of blacks and whites in which love and a family-in-Christ unity could be expressed in both word and action. The blacks who came to the farm had formerly been sharecroppers and now were no longer needed on the farms where they had worked. The white workers who came to the farm were courageous souls who shared Clarence's dream.

As might be expected in the Deep South in the mid- and late-1940s, opposition to the farm he set up was so great that some members of the "farm family" received numerous threats to their lives. The place was boycotted by other businesses, a fruit and vegetable stand was destroyed by crude bombing, and some of the members were beaten and jailed on trumped-up charges. Koinonians who were members of the local Baptist church were requested to leave that church. After all, those whites at Koinonia actually ate with black people!

But Clarence's dream of a Christian community never faded. Today, fifteen years after his death, Koinonia Farm (now called Koinonia Partners) is a flourishing Christian community. Thousands of visitors from all over the world visit each year. At least fifty houses have been built for people who could not otherwise afford one. Many workers can be found in the fields and in the pecan, candy, and clothing work areas on the farm.

Clarence Jordan was a farmer, preacher, author, and translator of the Bible. He even lectured in some of our country's most prestigious universities. His translation of Hebrews 11:1 expresses the heart of his thought and life. It reads, "Now faith is the turning of dreams into deeds; it is betting your life on the unseen realities."

At times Clarence was lonely. In a letter to me he wrote that one of the most difficult things about "being stuck off down here in southwest Georgia is the lack of any real stimulating, challenging conversation." But he used his loneliness creatively and productively. Even now, years after his death, his courageous example, his writings, and his translation of the New Testament into *The Cotton Patch Version* inspire thousands of others to turn dreams into deeds.

God intends that you have the courage to turn the pieces of your life, shattered by loneliness, into a whole new pattern of your dream, which you have timidly kept to yourself until now. What is your dream? Dare to put it into action. Exercise the wholehearted calling Christ has brought you!

Chapter 3

"I'm Bored to Death"

The Louisville Times Scene magazine recently published a three-page story on a current rock music star, John Cougar. Since his hometown is nearby Seymour, Indiana, the editors must have felt there would be a lot of reader interest in this local boy who had made good. However, what interested me more was how the theme of *boredom* permeated the attitude of John Cougar:

> He's fond of saying that, once you realize life is boring, you can learn to deal with it. It's a philosophy that plenty of young people understand. But at his concerts, especially those in Indiana and Kentucky, the kids know all the words to the songs John Cougar says are "meaningless." He is their champion, their chronicler, someone who understands.

The writer posed the question: How can a singer so busy and so successful still be plagued by doubts—and even boredom?

It is not difficult to find people who are bored. Recently, a college student home for the spring holidays placed a long-distance call to my son. I answered the phone and informed the young man that Jim was not at home just then but that I would be glad to take a message. The friend said, "Well, I'm bored to death and thought it would help if I could just talk to one of my classmates." He went on to explain that returning to his small, quiet Southern hometown after the excitement of having many friends and activities on a large university campus was a difficult transition to make. He felt there was nothing to do and no one to talk to. He was bored— "stimulus-deprived," as psychologists say.

No doubt you have, at times, been bored like this student. How would you describe the feeling? What do you say are the real causes of boredom? What are its symptoms and what kinds of boredom are there? And, finally, how do you cope with it? I suggested to the student in this situation that he seek out a needy family in that community, take them some groceries, and spend some time with them. (I never heard whether he tried this or just continued to talk about his boredom to anyone who would listen.)

What Is Boredom?

A bore is a dull person who keeps on talking when *you* want to talk! But what is boredom? Though boredom is one of the most common mental afflictions, it is difficult to find more than fifty papers published by scientists on the subject in the last half century. And books about boredom can be counted on one hand.

Boredom defies definition because it is a unique feeling. It intertwines with many other feelings and thus is difficult to isolate and understand. Some expressions connoting boredom are weariness, tedium, dull work, ennui, sameness, monotony, satiety, heavy hours, time on one's hands, doldrums, jadedness, apathy, lethargy, languor, lassitude, listlessness, detachment, indifference, lack of curiosity, unconcern. Quite a list, isn't it?

Actually, the word "boredom" is a relatively recent addition to the English language. It came into use about the middle of the eighteenth century. Its scope is limited largely to Western industrial society. Some definitions of boredom tie it directly to work. Thus boredom is an idea that seems to come from the machines of modern industrial society. In industry, to bore is to make a hole with a drill, to dig a well or a tunnel. This is the primary idea of the concept of boredom: being ground down, weariness, monotony.

I know something about this kind of boredom because, starting at age thirteen, I worked in a Southern cotton mill. At first I spread towels into fifty-pound bundles as they were cut from long strands of toweling material by a man with a huge steel cutting knife that was fastened to a table. From seven o'clock in the morning until five in the afternoon the towel cutter stood there in one spot, reached between the blades of that knife, pulled the towel strand to just the right position, and cut the towel from the strand. Competent cutters could cut a towel every three seconds.

After I was promoted from tying bundles, I was a towel cutter myself for almost six years. Standing in one area, I wore a hole through a solid oak floor doing repetitive work. It was the sort of work that dulls your emotional and mental sensitivities. Physically, it was demanding. I ended up with large varicose veins in my legs. Habits formed then still prompt me to produce each day some tangible evidence that I have put in some work that day, a visible sign that I have completed something. I recall how in 1935, when the eight-hour day went into effect, I was able to leave my job at three in the afternoon instead of five o'clock (after having gone to work at seven in the morning). I can still remember the ecstasy I felt when the warmth of the bright sun enveloped me. Why, I was sure the kingdom of God had come right then and there! But halfway home I suddenly had a deep sense of guilt, for here it was broad daylight and I wasn't working! After fifty years out of the mills, I still have occasional nightmares about trying to escape from there. For, indeed, I was caught in what seemed to be an endless grinding, monotonous, boring work situation.

What Is Your Brand of Boredom?

There are different degrees of boredom. Simple boredom hits us all, now and then. A lack of challenging stimuli or meaningful activity may cause it. Not only adults but children also may be victims of this sort of boredom. For example, little Will was in nursery school and there was some question about his being "promoted" to kindergarten, because he seemed nonchalant and unresponsive to questions by his teacher. His concerned parents secured two experts in child guidance to test little Will's I.Q. and to visit his class to observe. They discovered that the lad was exceptionally bright and that he didn't respond to questions by the teacher because he was bored. He knew the answers, but the questions no longer stimulated him intellectually.

I think I know how little Will felt. I was forced into the first grade but learned to like it because the teacher showed every pupil some personal attention. The second grade turned me against all teachers because I was punished for something with which I had nothing to do. I cannot for my life remember being in the third. The fourth grade was a disaster. After I spent two years at that level, the teacher decided that she could take no more and handed me over to the fifth grade. There I learned only two basic things, but those things have served as guiding principles of my life. I had to stay in after school one day and memorize the Hundredth Psalm before I could go home. It took only minutes. The other thing I learned was a statement from *The Spectator* in which the old gentleman farmer, Sir Roger de Coverley, observes, "There is much to be said on both sides of every issue." Years later, after I became a Christian, I learned to praise and thank God like the psalmist. And Sir Roger de Coverley's motto became mine, especially in teaching Christian ethics. I always tried to present both sides of an issue and let the students make their own decisions. In 1961, for example, I brought in the local chairman of the White Citizens Council to address a class I was teaching, and then I invited Martin Luther King, Jr., to lecture.

In the sixth grade, the teacher tried to force me to keep my fiery red hair combed and parted in the middle and to wear a tie. (I discovered later that she was in love with the principal of the public school, who wore a tie and parted *his* hair in the middle. She later married him.) But I refused to wear the ties the teacher gave me. Finally, she kept me in after school and informed me that I would never amount to anything and should get out of school. But I stayed with it and she promoted me to the seventh grade, where I lasted about two weeks. One day in class, when I was daydreaming, the professor (in those days male teachers were called professors) asked me who wrote Poe's "Raven." Jolted out of my dreamworld, I replied, "I don't know." The whole class burst out laughing. I never went back. Was it boredom? Was it lack of motivation? Was it humiliation? Was it anger? Boredom is intertwined with all of these.

Six years later, I went back to school in another town. The principal asked which grade I wanted to attend. I picked the ninth grade. It was a real challenge. Try doing second-year algebra without having learned simple fractions. But the rest of high school was never boring. I had a lot of catching up to do and a powerful motivation: a call to the ministry.

Simple boredom during those school years could have been overcome with a more challenging school curriculum and a few caring teachers. The same could be said of schools today. Unfortunately, our teachers are burdened with so many trivial tasks and with such large classes that they cannot teach effectively. Indeed, the public school system in this country appears to be structured so as to prevent teachers from teaching and students from learning. It is a symptom of the epidemic of boredom in our society. You will notice that fads in education are quickly adopted and just as quickly discarded. The latest fad, that of computerizing the classroom, is no guarantee that more learning will take place or even that children will be more eager to learn. In fact, in early 1983 the Associated Press wire service carried a story about experiments in which a chimpanzee was to be taught how to manipulate a particular computer terminal. The experimenter reported, "We figured it would take two to two and a half weeks, but he had it down in the first five minutes. Within fifteen minutes, he was thoroughly bored with us."

Ordinary or garden variety boredom is always in danger of becoming chronic boredom. "Chronic" means continuing for a long time. This means having boredom with you for months or even years. This second major kind of boredom may be due to your inability to respond to stimuli. If this is the case, boredom may have become a way of life for you that need not be. You can see this in people who refuse to change for the better and simply accept things as they are.

One morning a man who was an employee of the hospital ate breakfast with me in the cafeteria there. He described, three times without stopping, his daily routine. "I get up, dress, eat breakfast, go to work, do my job, go home, eat dinner, watch TV, go to bed." It became boring just listening to the dull repetition. I could feel my eyes glazing over and I recalled the boring dialogue in the film *Marty,* where the two friends are trying to decide on their evening activities.

> "Well, whaddaya' wanna do, Angie?"
> "I dunno. What do *you* wanna do?"
> "Aw, I dunno. What about you?"
> "I dunno, Marty."

It was hard not to yawn, and I realized this man had lost his passion for life, like T. S. Eliot's character J. Alfred Prufrock, who laments, "I have measured out my life with coffee spoons."

Chronic boredom can be distinguished from ordinary boredom in that it lasts longer and does not always change with the changing situation. You feel trapped and sense a lack of freedom. But you still have a vague hope that things might get better. You can still function, but not with full capacity and efficiency. Your sleep pattern may prevent you from getting needed rest and relaxation. In this condition, your boredom could easily degenerate into depression, in which you may despair of life itself.

Boredom and Brokenness

The medical consequences of boredom have never been thoroughly researched. Findings so far, however, clearly show a connection between physical and mental health and boredom. Some surveys of the physical effects of boredom have been made. In Australia, for example, telegraphers were studied in comparison with clerical, maintenance, and supervisory personnel in the same office. Results showed that telegraphers, whose work was more monotonous, were more likely to suffer more frequently from asthma, bronchitis, hand tremors, heavy drinking, and excessive smoking (J. F. O'Hanlon, "Boredom: Practical Consequences and a Theory," *Acta Psychologica* 49, 1981, pp. 53–82).

Mentally and emotionally, the bored tend to be more neurotic and less healthy mentally. Feelings of resentment and repressed hostility are evident, along with feelings of depression. And there is strong evidence that monotonous work reduces the worker's intelligence (p. 65). This means that repetitive work cuts down on your efficiency.

Avoiding the Casualties of Boredom

The chief casualties of boredom are love, curiosity, will and enthusiasm, and a sense of wonder. Boredom tends to erase these qualities and replace them with indifference.

Avoiding such losses is of intense importance to your productive living and mine.

The Hazards of Boredom to Love

The opposite of love is not hate but insensitivity or indifference. Hate does recognize others as persons. To the insensitive individual, you are a thing. If you are insensitive to another person, you are unresponsive, unmoved, and narcotized to your neighbor as a human being.

Today, many people are trapped in marriages in which spouses are treated as things; their value is one of utility. As a pastoral counselor, I deal with many such cases. Mary, for example, is the wife of Paul, a graduate student about to receive his Ph.D. Mary tells me that she has worked as a secretary for the past five years to help keep Paul in college and professional school. They were married during his senior year in college. Now Paul tells her that he no longer loves her, that she bores him, and that he wants a divorce. He has found someone more stimulating and exciting, someone whom he has been counseling. Such examples show up in marriages of medical, law, and theological students and other professionals where the wife has supported the husband through school but lacked opportunity to grow along with him. More recently, we have occasionally seen the reverse, a husband being discarded after he has put his wife through school! When the wife or husband's usefulness wears out, she or he is abandoned (along with the kids, if there are any) for a mate worthy of the newly acquired status of the spouse.

The Hazards of Boredom to Curiosity

Boredom is the withdrawal of curiosity. You have heard the old saw, "Curiosity killed the cat." But you are not a cat! You are a person and cannot really live well without curiosity. "Check it out," we say; this is a healthy attitude. Moses in the desert, taking care of his father-in-law's sheep, saw a burning bush that was not consumed. "I will turn aside," he said, "and see this great sight, why the bush is not burnt" (Ex. 3:3). When Moses did so, God commissioned him to set the Israelites free from political bondage in Egypt. God speaks to the investigative mind and shares his mission in the world with those who turn aside and see.

Centuries later another Jew, Albert Einstein, was asked by a student for a word of wisdom, a guiding principle of life. The scientist's answer: "Never lose your holy curiosity." This is the principle laid down by the apostle Paul for the early Christians: "Test everything; hold fast what is good" (I Thess. 5:21). Jesus himself commanded his hearers to love God with the "mind" as well as the heart and the soul (Luke 10:25–28). This certainly implies that you can be intelligent and a Christian at the same time.

The Hazards of Boredom to Will and Enthusiasm

Boredom destroys your will to think, act, and live adventurously. You give in to the desire to leave things as they are. People who do things are individuals with strong wills. Boredom strangles the will and makes you impotent, indifferent, unmovable. Great and good things are willed instead of merely wished. You know that one of the signs of recovery from great sadness or despair is the exercise of the will—the will to live, to love, and to find meaning. You begin to exercise initiative again.

One middle-aged woman had been hospitalized for deep depression. She felt her life had lost its meaning since her divorce. She was showing little response to the medical staff or her surroundings. She was allowed to spend a weekend with her sister and her sister's children. Since it was close to Christmas, the woman—childless herself—was asked by the youngsters to help wrap presents. At first she was hesitant, but the enthusiasm of the youngsters spilled over until she was soon happily showing them how to tie fancy bows and fold neat corners on the package wrappings. Her doctor was amazed at her progress upon her return to the hospital; she began to participate more actively in the crafts and structured programs, which helped speed her recovery of her own will.

Several years ago, a dedicated schoolteacher was forced to retire at age sixty-five. She knew she would be "bored at home in a rocking chair" and decided, "I've got a lot of mileage left in me yet!" So she secured a teaching job in a neighboring county where the mandatory retirement age was seventy. For five years that teacher rose early in the morning and drove 22 miles to teach retarded children. "I love those children and they love me," she insisted. "They need me *almost* as much as I need them!"

Retirement from a job seems to be a period of restlessness and boredom if the retiree hasn't planned ahead for filling those nonemployed hours. Perhaps you have noticed how many letters are sent to advice columnists asking, "What can I do about my husband (or wife) being around constantly now that he (or she) is retired?" Even workers who have spent their adulthood making decisions and giving instructions to co-workers often have difficulty ordering their own retirement time into a meaningful pattern. "I just can't find anything to *do*," they complain. We'll look at this problem again in Chapter 6.

The Hazards of Boredom to the Sense of Wonder

A sense of wonder is always a casualty of boredom. Once I heard a lecture by the French philosopher, Jacques Maritain in which he pointed out that modern philosophers have lost a sense of wonder in our technologically structured society. He pleaded for the recovery of a sense of wonder. We of the West have for a long time witnessed the demise of wonder and yet wistfully desire its return. The nostalgic and perhaps unconscious yearning of children for the faith of their fathers is poignantly expressed by the poet Thomas Hood, who early in life thought that the tops of the fir trees reached up to heaven. In his older years he had lost such simple wonder and "childish ignorance":

> Now 'tis little joy
> To know I'm farther off from heaven
> Than when I was a boy.

Immanuel Kant is one philosopher who did not lose his sense of wonder. At the conclusion of his *Critique of Practical Reason,* he confesses, "Two things fill the heart with ever renewed and increasing wonderment and reverence: the starry firmament above me and the moral law within me."

Wonder is that which arouses astonishment, curiosity, and admiration. This quality is possessed by little children. Jesus makes it one of the essentials for entrance into the kingdom of God. It is a quality necessary for learning. One of my college professors used to say that in order to learn the truth we must stand in the presence of mystery with the wonder of a little child. By this he meant that we must have a sense of openness to the truth. Boredom strips us of such an attitude, interfering with awe and the reception of reality.

Battling Boredom

Boredom is not an easy prison to break out of. You have to do battle against it. Nietzsche said, "Against boredom even the gods themselves struggle in vain." But the struggle is not always in vain. Ways of beating boredom have been devised.

Name the Demon

One name for boredom is *acedia.* The strange word comes from the Greek words meaning "not caring" (*a,* not; *kēdos,* care). The early Christian theologians considered it one of the seven deadly sins. It is closely akin to sloth, dejection, and boredom. John Cassian, in the fifth century, described the danger it presents to those who dwell in the desert. It

comes like a fever and is identified with "the midday de-
mons" spoken of in Psalm 91:6.

So the first step in coping with boredom is to *name* it—that
is, to learn something about it and admit that you have it.
Find out the sources of your boredom. What kind of boredom has trapped you, simple or chronic? Name the demon.
Until the doctor diagnoses the disease, he cannot control it
and the patient cannot relax. If you cannot "name the demon," you cannot control it.

Until you check yourself out, you are not likely to get beyond boredom. For boredom can work like an opiate to tran-
quilize you against escaping the torment of tedium. It dead-
ens your will and narcotizes you against a breakthrough.

Rotate Your Routine

The nineteenth-century theologian and philosopher Søren
Kierkegaard suggests that "rotation" (a farming term) is a
way of escaping boredom. This is not a change of field but
of crop and of the mode of cultivation. Kierkegaard is serious. For him, "boredom is the root of all evil" *(Either/Or).*
Whether or not you accept Kierkegaard's theological idea of
boredom, his practical principle of rotation is helpful.

Rotation certainly pays off in farming. In the South, when
"cotton was king," the boll weevil crossed over from Mexico
to the United States and destroyed the cotton plants. Farmers were forced to grow a variety of crops, such as soybeans
and peanuts. They learned to use their land to raise cattle,
hogs, and chickens. As a result, many more farmers became
prosperous than in the days when only cotton was grown.

The people of Enterprise, Alabama, were so grateful for
what had occurred that in 1910 they erected a monument to
the boll weevil. For when they turned from the single-crop
system to diversified farming, they became wealthier. The inscription on the monument reads: "In profound appreciation
of the boll weevil and what it has done to herald prosper-
ity."

Here are some practical "rotations" you can make to reduce your boredom.

1. Take up walking, jogging, or running; all are good exercise and will help in getting rid of your frustrations.

2. Start a new hobby: juggling, wood carving, painting, gourmet cooking, ceramics. Join a class to learn new skills.

3. Learn to dance. Square dancing, clogging, and other kinds of dancing aid in meeting new friends and are good, wholesome exercise.

4. Take the plunge and form some new friendships. Sometimes you get bored with an ever-shrinking circle of friends. Expand the circle.

5. Get some training in meditation. This is a lost art among Americans. Memorize inspiring passages of the Bible.

6. Take a bus ride all around your town and see where your neighbors live, without having to keep your eyes glued to a freeway as you would if you drove.

7. Form a small group dedicated to showing careful and loving consideration of each other and to thinking and acting on the promotion of justice in the community.

8. Visit the local prison, jail, or hospital and talk with prisoners and patients about their problems.

9. At Christmas time, instead of buying gifts for your friends, create some thoughtful gifts and letters for them and use your gift money to send a donation to CARE or another charity in their names.

10. Sit down and write that letter you have planned for a long time, pick up the phone and call, or cook a special dish to share with a friend who may be recovering from an illness or living alone.

11. Help find a job for some unemployed person.

12. Plant a garden.

13. Develop a reading program of your own. Ask for help in this from your pastor, a teacher friend, or another friend who loves books.

14. Link your life with a cause that is worth giving your life for.

15. Make up your *own* list of boredom-fighting ideas and talk them over with your family and friends.

People who sit around and wait for life to supply their satisfactions almost always end up with boredom.

Discover the Benefits of Boredom

Boredom is not all bad. It can either pacify or push you. It can push you into different, and sometimes new, activities and ways of thinking. Blessed are you if you can turn boredom into new ways of doing things.

Some go so far as to claim that boredom—rather than physical and social needs—lies at the very roots of humanity's spiritual progress. It certainly prods some people to break the boundaries of ordinary existence and move toward greater knowledge in all areas of life.

By trying to see the value of boredom, you can tolerate it better. If your life were all stimulation, the result would be boredom with the overstimulated life.

Contemplate and Seek to Understand Mystery

As long as you are trying to understand various mysteries, creating something of beauty, or seeking truth, you will experience little boredom. Have you noticed that some of the most alert and interesting older people are those who keep their clue-hunting skills sharpened by doing crossword puzzles, playing games, or even reading mysteries like those of Agatha Christie? Such people continue to maintain an interest in what is going on at the national and international levels and try also to unlock real-life mysteries, not just fictional ones. They continue trying to make sense of bewildering circumstances, seeking answers not only to crossword puzzles but also to the profound questions about the meaning of life and death.

Climb from Pit to Power

You may have said sometime, "Boredom is the pits." This is a current slang expression; it is also a biblical insight. In the Bible, "the Pit" often refers figuratively to feelings of boredom, depression, and powerlessness. For example, in Psalm 28:1 we read about those "who go down to the Pit." The writer of Psalm 88 speaks of being powerless, feeling cut off, forgotten. The Pit is "dark and deep" (v. 6), and the psalmist is "shut in so that I cannot escape" (v. 8). This is psychological language and does not specifically identify the illness; but it provides, as Walter Brueggemann observes, "a marvelous receptacle which we are free to fill with our particular experiences" (*Praying the Psalms,* p. 42; St. Mary's Press, 1982).

The Psalms can be an antidote to boredom. Psalm 42 has the ladder by which you can climb out of the Pit. "Why are you cast down, O my soul?" (vs. 5, 11). So the first rung in the ladder leading up out of the Pit is self-communion. When boredom settles in, you should talk to your self or your soul. Ask yourself why you are downcast. Learn something about yourself. As the ancient Greeks advised, "Know yourself." You will be surprised at the self you observe. You may discover that you are boring yourself by limiting your ways of relating to other people, or by the things you do to, for, and with them.

So, being forced by "the Pit experience" (we'll discuss this again in Chapter 6) to search out truth in ourselves and in sacred writings, we can continue up the ladder.

Memory and imagination can help us manage boredom. "My soul is cast down within me, therefore I remember thee" (Ps. 42:6). Viktor Frankl declares that remembrance of earlier happy experiences helped him to survive the horrors of Hitler's concentration camps. In my own life, fantasizing about what I knew I could never be or enjoy helped me survive six years of repetitive work in the cotton mill. I turned on my inner movie and saw myself in a Western, a mystery, or a gangster scene. John did not have movies or television, but he did use his vivid imagination when he was exiled on the island of Patmos and wrote the book of Revelation. That book's theme is the ultimate triumph of Christ and his disciples against radical evil.

"Hope in God" (Ps. 42:5, 11) is the chief thing the psalmist keeps telling his soul. All through the Bible, God is recognized as the hope of the world, the "God of hope" (Rom. 15:13). Hoping in God never disappoints and can lift you out of the pit of despair to a sense of power.

One morning I stopped by the hospital room of a patient who had suffered extensive paralyzing injuries because of a bad fall. She was able to move only her left arm and hand. With that one useful hand she struggled to open her New Testament to Romans 5; then she read aloud, "We rejoice in our sufferings, knowing that suffering produces endurance, and endurance produces character, and character produces hope, and hope does not disappoint us, because God's love has been poured into our hearts through the Holy Spirit which has been given to us" (Rom. 5:3–5). Her hope, in the midst of very bleak circumstances, was grounded in God. Her view from the Pit was not one of despair; rather, she had the hope of power far beyond her near-helpless condition. Although I was supposed to be cheering her up, it was the patient who was indeed the minister!

A Danger to Our World

It would be interesting to research how many important events in human history resulted from boredom. According to some accounts, Nero instigated the burning of Rome because of boredom; Alexander the Great wept because he had no more worlds to conquer; the mind of genius Leonardo da Vinci was racked with boredom in his princely surroundings during his final years. Boredom can have powerful adverse effects on people and, through them, on the world.

Bertrand Russell declared of boredom, "At least half the sins of mankind are caused by the fear of it" (*The Conquest of Happiness,* p. 40; Avon Book Co., 1930). So we engage in wars, persecutions, pogroms, and other forms of violence to find excitement and diversion from boredom.

A Harvard scholar, Harlow Shapley, made up a list of "possible causes of the destruction of civilization." On this list he included nuclear war, natural catastrophe, and widespread disease. Ranked *third* on this list is—you guessed it—boredom! To avoid this sort of disaster, said Bertrand Russell, "means must be found of restoring individual initiative not only in things that are trivial but in the things that really matter."

Boredom, then, is a common affliction of humanity. You can cope with it if you accept it as a fact of life and act to deal with it. Break out of your boredom by changing your routine, using your imagination, and finding a purpose in life that consumes all there is of you.

Chapter 4

"I Am So Anxious"

She was an attractive woman in her late twenties. Her room in the hospital was orderly and her clothes and books were neatly put in their proper places. She was well groomed and tastefully dressed. On the surface, she didn't appear to have any problems at all. (I had, however, come to see her at the request of her psychiatrist.) When I asked if she knew why she was in the clinic, her reply was, "I'm so anxious, so afraid. Why do I operate on fear instead of love in my Christian life?" She continued by saying she had read an article in the newspaper stating that Christ would return on a specific date in the near future. As that predicted date drew near, this patient was becoming more anxious and fearful. Her inner distress had shattered the wholeness of her being, and her illness was the painful result.

You and I are more like than unlike this woman in her fretfulness. Anxiety in different degrees appears to be prevalent in—or native to—all human beings. Stress causes anxiety to increase, and some persons, like this woman, are overwhelmed by it. As Thoreau wrote in *Walden,* "The mass of men lead lives of quiet desperation."

The 1940s were characterized by the poet W. H. Auden as an "Age of Anxiety." Today, many people depend upon medications to put their shaky nerves at ease and to quiet their nameless fears. However, some experts in the use of these medications say that their effectiveness is very short-lived, lasting two weeks on an average! In well-practiced medicine, their main benefits would be for people with orthopedic injuries, muscular spasms, threatened seizures, and the like. These experts say that the optimal long-term handling of anxiety involves not medications but changing one's way of life through self-understanding, the refocusing of one's main concerns and loyalties, and the practice of relaxation rituals, physical exercise, and meditation. An increasing number of physicians add contemplation and prayer.

In this discussion, therefore, we will address ourselves to the long-term rather than the quick-fix or short-term approaches to and uses of anxiety. Some anxiety is runaway creativity, wrongly directed concern, inaccurately placed fear. We will see how to harness its energies, redirect its concerns, and accurately aim its fears to those things which need to be feared, so that your best interests, and those of your loved ones, may be fulfilled in the kingdom of God and the image of Christ.

This chapter is designed to help you not only understand and cope with anxiety but also use it to your advantage and for the benefit of others. You need to be aware of the forms and expressions of this feeling, along with the sources from which it comes. You cannot get completely free of anxiety and you would not want to, because it is a real sign that you are sensitive to and concerned about your world. You can, however, find ways of mobilizing your anxiety through the Christian faith by following some practical guidelines and having clear purposes in life.

A Working Understanding of Anxiety

Although you can sense its effects, anxiety is very difficult to explain. It is commonly described as a feeling of fearful uneasiness or apprehension, as over some impending or anticipated event, or as uneasiness and distress about future uncertainties. Physicians define anxiety generally as fear or dread without a clear cause or a specific threat. One cause of anxiety is noticing one's first gray hair. Other causes include facing surgery, going off to college for the first time, starting a new job, moving the family to an unfamiliar town or city, and waiting for test results. These instances are filled with uncertainty and can be extremely anxious times.

It is necessary to distinguish between fear and anxiety. In the case of fear, the threat or danger is obvious and specific. For example, you may fear a specific dog that you encounter daily while walking or jogging. Anxiety, on the other hand, is more subjective; it is hidden inside you and not attached to any particular thing. It is "free floating." For example, if someone casually mentions dogs, you become anxious, yet no dogs are present! In short, fear is directly related to a special object; anxiety fails to discern its object.

The Bible discusses anxiety with different but very familiar words. Jesus said to his disciples that in this world they would have "tribulation"—that is, they would be under pressure (John 16:33). So you and I live in a world of anxiety. Paul speaks of being in "anguish" (II Cor. 2:4). Jesus himself, in thinking about his crucifixion and death, declared that he was "constrained," "pressed with anguish," until his mission was accomplished (Luke 12:50).

The Bible provides a positive, creative, and caring other side to anxiety. It talks about "genuine" anxiety. This is concern about the welfare of others; it means caring for others, taking their best interests to heart, and doing the works of love toward them. It recognizes anxiety as being both unproductive fretfulness, on the one hand, and productive concern for great causes and needy people, on the other. Both provide an overall working understanding of anxiety that can help you shape a strategy for turning the adversities of anxiety into advantages.

Forms of Anxiety

Anxiety comes in several forms, but for our purpose we shall look at three: chronic, common, and creative.

Chronic Anxiety

Chronic anxiety is the unhealthy kind. It persistently plagues you. Paul Tillich identifies this type as pathological anxiety. It threatens you with nonbeing, meaninglessness, and moral condemnation. Therefore it is counterproductive to the healthy life. Chronic anxiety may require professional treatment.

Common Anxiety

This kind of anxiety is often referred to as existential and is common to all of us. The apostle Paul refers to it when he says, "No temptation has overtaken you that is not common to man" (I Cor. 10:13). It stems from your sense of finiteness or human limitations. You realize that you can't do everything you want to. As you get older, you think about what you have not accomplished and you know you will never be able to achieve some of your goals. You begin to realize that time is running out and that it will all end and you will depart to that country from which no traveler returns.

Creative Anxiety

Our concern in dealing with chronic anxiety has caused us to overlook anxiety's positive role. It can alert us and prompt us to do our duty. As a student, you no doubt found yourself under the pressure of final exams. Your anxiety about passing a course forced you to cram until the wee hours of the morning. But you probably passed the course and learned some things along the way—including the need to plan a better program of study for the next exam time!

Anxiety about the possibility of developing cancer or heart disease or losing sight or hearing can send you to your doctor, who may discover the beginning of a problem and solve it.

Anxiety can be a positive common factor in your growth. Going away to college can fill you with anxiety. But once you are through the first semester, the anxiety subsides. You understand the situation better, friends provide support, and the terror of tests declines. A child watches with anxiety while others jump into the swimming pool. As his or her turn comes closer, the anxiety becomes more intense. But once the child has taken the plunge, usually there is a great sense of relief and achievement.

Older people experience anxiety when they undertake new responsibilities. A newly widowed woman in her late forties had to find employment after years of being a competent housewife. Her secretarial skills were a bit rusty, but she was confident she could bring them up to date—until she was shown her new work area. There were sleek, complicated computers for various tasks, very different surroundings from the familiar office settings she remembered, new faces to recognize and names to remember, new ways of doing things. Her hands shook and she left work each day with a splitting headache for the first few weeks. "But I decided," she said later, "that if all the others in the office had been able to learn to use those machines and master the situation, I could too. I'm really not *that* dumb. I just tried to master one thing at a time, rather than biting off the whole chunk."

Signs of Anxiety

How much attention have you given to understanding your own anxiety? What are its signs? Generalized ongoing anxiety is manifested in many ways. Sometimes it takes the form of specific behaviors. Among these are muscular tensions, muscle aches, inability to relax, tiredness, eyelid twitch, fidgeting, restlessness, shallow breathing, tightened fists, nail-biting, sweaty palms, and hand-wringing. Anxiety may show up in physical symptoms. These can include severe blushing, increased heart rate, dry mouth, tightening of the voice, dizziness, tingling in hands and feet, upset stomach, hot and cold spells, diarrhea, loss of appetite, and restless sleep. When you are anxious, breathing becomes more difficult. The German word for anxiety is *Angst,* from the Latin *angustia:* narrowness of space, shortness. Note that when you are anxious you should breathe long, deeply, and regularly. Take a brief break from your task and go somewhere nearby where it is quiet. Compose yourself. This will help you to deal with your anxiety on the spot.

Some Causes of Your Being Anxious

Rapid and Repeated Change
In our radically changing society, anxiety has become a part of everyday life. Alvin Toffler in *Future Shock* observed that change is so rapid that our moral, psychological, and religious lives have not been able to keep pace. This situation, of course, creates anxiety. It may also have an organic, or physical, basis. For example, there may be anxiety attacks due to the excessive drinking of alcohol or caffeinated beverages or to the abuse of drugs.

Separation
Separation is especially hard for children, since they depend on parents for love and security. John Bowlby made a study of children separated from their parents or parent substitutes. The children went through the process of protest and then of detachment. These were their ways of coping with the anxiety involved in separation. They became increasingly self-centered and, instead of directing their feelings toward people, became preoccupied with material things

such as sweets, toys, and food (*Attachment,* Vol. I, pp. 28–29; Basic Books, 1969).

Shifts in Your Station in Life

Leaving the security of home to go to school can be a stressful time for the young child, who often acts out that anxiety by throwing tantrums or retreating into extreme shyness. Also, young people become anxious when they seek full-time employment after completing their schooling. Parents often become more anxious than their children when the children go away from home—to attend college, enter the service, find employment, or make homes of their own. Sometimes a promotion from one job to another can produce anxiety for the worker. Likewise, older people facing retirement become anxious because of the impending changes facing them.

Religion *can* be a source of security. The wrong kind of religion can create common anxiety and even turn it into pathological anxiety. This is the legalistic and fear-driven religion of which Freud spoke and which he rejected. Yet Harry Emerson Fosdick said rightly, "What Freud called religion Jesus called sin." This religion is the kind of nit-picking obedience to minor morals that Jesus condemned in leaders who bound heavy burdens, and laid them on people, but did not lift one finger to help bear them. It makes what a Mississippi farmer called "an unnecessary conscience." His elementary-school-age daughter was terrified of returning to school when she found a forgotten piece of chalk in her dress pocket. She feared that the teacher would be angry with her and punish her for stealing! Her father said, "I believe in right and wrong and that stealing is wrong, but her heart is loaded down with an unnecessary conscience."

You may be plagued by the burden of unnecessary scruples, which shatter your wholeness with a nameless anxiety. You may have let this burden spread to the whole world.

Religious Threat

You may feel that you have not been or cannot be forgiven, or that you have committed "the unpardonable sin." You may be anxious about the end of the world and the coming of Christ in judgment. You may be so anxious about death that you cannot enjoy a life that is presently joyous. I often see persons who have deep anxiety about death. When they tell me that death is one of their fears, I extend my hand with a smile and say, "Join the club." It is for freedom from such fears that Christ sets us free. They are a yoke of bondage, but his yoke is easy and his burden is light. His resurrection takes this study of blind anxiety out of death and gives you and me a hope that does not disappoint.

New Responsibilities

There is also the anxiety, mentioned before, about whether you have what it takes to do the job you are hired to do. I am aware that ministers, as they get older, often feel out of touch with their church responsibilities. Much of the training they received at seminary decades ago appears to be irrelevant. Since they have not kept up with their studies, they feel insecure and become discouraged and depressed.

Indecision

Inability to make a decision is a basic source of anxiety. It can result in a neurotic or unhealthy anxiety. Dante presented a dramatic picture of acute anxiety in victims of indecisiveness. The first group he met on entering hell were the indecisive persons, "the wretched souls of those who could never make up their minds" (*Inferno*, III). These were neutral people who could not make moral decisions.

Some persons depend on others to make decisions for them. They prefer not to make choices but to allow others to decide for them. If there is no one to decide for them, they feel lost and become very anxious.

War and Rumors of War

The threat of nuclear war can be a strong source of anxiety. A flood of "fear books" has recently flowed from the presses. Serious debate about nuclear war is in process. For the first time in history a few people—politicians, power-hungry leaders, and technicians—have the power to destroy civilization.

As a result, a cloud of fear has settled over the world. Children are aware of and anxious about the possibility of nuclear war. Amy Carter tells her father, President Jimmy Carter, that nuclear war is one of the great issues facing humankind. Samantha Smith, elementary school pupil, writes Yuri Andropov of the Soviet Union about stopping the arms race, "If you don't want war and we don't want war, then why do we go on making nuclear bombs?"

Anxiety can focus on a whole cluster of concrete things. For example, you may fear losing your job, business, home, or savings. I vividly recall that, during the Depression of the 1930s, cars, homes, furniture, farms, and many other things of value were reclaimed by lending agencies because those who had bought them on credit couldn't pay for them.

Jesus' Concern About Your Anxiety

Jesus talks about anxiety states and also about the creative uses of anxiety. He deals with an anxiety disorder that is ignored by most therapists: the specific anxiety about, the obsession or desire for, material things. It is manifested particularly in anxiety about what we shall eat, drink, and wear as described in the Sermon on the Mount (Matt. 6:19–34).

Economic Anxiety

Jesus warns his followers against being overly anxious about things, as the Gentiles are. (The term "Gentiles" is used in the New Testament in reference to those who are not Jewish [Luke 21:24] or in contrast to the followers of Christ [Matt. 6:7, 32; 10:5; 20:19].) The life-style of the Gentiles differed from that of the disciples. Gentiles greeted their brethren only (Matt. 5:47); prayed in a loud voice in public (Matt. 6:5); were "darkened in their understanding" and separated from the life of God (Eph. 4:18); were given to idolatry (I Cor. 10:20) and immorality (I Cor. 5:1); and sought after material things (Matt. 6:32; Luke 12:30).

Jesus refers to the Gentiles' overanxiousness about material things in Matt. 6:25–34:

> Therefore I tell you, do not be anxious about your life, what you shall eat or what you shall drink, nor about your body, what you shall put on. Is not life more than food, and the body more than clothing? Look at the birds of the air: they neither sow nor reap nor gather into barns, and yet your heavenly Father feeds them. Are you not of more value than they? And which of you by being anxious can add one cubit to his span of life? And why are you anxious about clothing? Consider the lilies of the field, how they grow; they neither toil nor spin; yet I tell you, even Solomon in all his glory was not arrayed like one of these. But if God so clothes the grass of the field, which today is alive and tomorrow is thrown into the oven, will he not much more clothe you, O men of little faith? Therefore do not be anxious, saying, "What shall we eat?" or "What shall we drink?" or "What shall we wear?" For the Gentiles seek all these things; and your heavenly Father knows that you need them all. But seek first his kingdom and his righteousness, and all these things shall be yours as well.

Here is one of the most penetrating statements ever uttered about anxiety. Yet it is rarely, if ever, referred to by psychiatrists and counselors in dealing with anxious people. I have attended many conferences on psychopharmacology and anxiety, but I have yet to hear a reference made to Jesus' view of anxiety and how to cope with it

The Greek word Jesus uses six times in the above passage is *merimnaō,* which means to strive after, to be unduly concerned about things like food and clothing, as the Gentiles were. But while this tendency of the Gentiles is to be condemned, we must take a look at our own hankering for things.

Augustine declared that you can measure the character of a nation by the way it spends its money. In our own nation we anxiously spend billions of dollars for armaments, including nuclear weapons. The Stockholm International Research Institute declares that the world spent $500 billion, more than $1 million per minute, in 1980 for arms. Our own annual military budget is moving toward the $1 trillion mark. The obscene amounts of money spent in the United States on clothes, food, cars, alcohol, and drugs bear witness to our obsession with escaping our anxiety by means of things, possessions, and the status we want to think (in our insecurity) they bring us.

"Things are in the saddle and ride mankind," wrote Emerson in his "Ode to W. H. Channing." Many people have lost a realistic sense of values. A country music maker lives in a $14 million home. A guru's gullible followers provide him with twenty-four Rolls-Royce automobiles. An oil magnate has a castle in Europe and a half dozen other mansions around the world. You can think of many other examples—and some of them might be in your own neighborhood—of status and things being of primary importance to people. But I am convinced that in a world where millions of people live with hunger, starvation, poverty, and inadequate medical care, such thing-based life-styles are obscene. (An accumulation of things out of proportion to need is a surplus. And your surplus—or mine—is someone else's subsistence.)

But underneath all this showy affluence, anxiety about things gnaws away. A very intelligent and genteel lady lived in a large house in a small Southern town. Haunted by the memory of her family's losing a fortune during Depression days, she began to save, as she got older, everything she could. She hoarded newspapers, canned goods (some of which were decades old), jars, scraps of food, paper, ribbons, boxes, and bows, until you could get through the big rooms in her house only by narrow paths. Her problem was insecurity and not being willing to suffer loss again. She thought that the accumulation of things—no matter how trivial—would reduce her anxiety.

At the root of greed is anxiety. Paul the apostle says that "the love of money is the root of all evils" (I Tim. 6:10). The love of money here means a craving for it. This is idolatry. Jesus made it clear that "you cannot serve God and mammon" (Matt. 6:24). The word "mammon" means money, riches. You are a divided person if you try to serve both. While you cannot serve God *and* money, you can serve God *with* money. But you cannot have it both ways. For then you will become "double-minded" (James 1:8; 4:8). John Bunyan called such a character "Mr. Facing-both-ways."

The Contemplation of Nature

The first step in dealing with your anxiety is to commune with nature. Consider the birds and the flowers, Jesus suggested in Matthew 6. "Look at the birds"—they neither sow nor reap, yet God takes care of them. This doesn't mean that they never work. "Consider the lilies"—they neither toil nor spin, yet God takes care of them; they grow without anxiety. If the birds of the air and the lilies of the field are thus provided for, human beings, made in the image of God, can certainly count on God's care. Relief from anxiety may so affect your body as to add to the length of your life. A study of hundred-year-old people shows that seven out of eleven factors relating to their longevity had to do with the elimination of worry.

Jesus' first therapeutic prescription for anxiety, then, is to look at nature and trust the God who created and sustains all things. In this, Jesus echoes the ancient truth that nature has healing qualities. One of Job's friends advises him, in all his suffering, to consider God's marvelous ways in nature (Job 37). Then the Lord answers Job "out of the whirlwind" (Job 38:1). The psalmist was aware of the revelation of God in nature. He exclaims, "The heavens are telling the glory of God" (Ps. 19:1). Such awareness reduces our anxiety and assures us that God is still in control of the universe and our personal lives.

Priorities

Of course, Jesus nowhere discounts forethought and planning about material things. "For which of you, desiring to build a tower, does not first sit down and count the cost, whether he has enough to complete it?" (Luke 14:28). Jesus does teach that material things must be subordinate to the kingdom of God. "But seek first his kingdom and his righteousness, and all these things shall be yours as well" (Matt. 6:33). Thus the kingdom of God calls for the rearrangement of your priorities.

God's kingdom demands love, justice, humility, and service to human need, and in our personal lives it takes top priority. When Olin Binkley was a student at Wake Forest College, his finances were exhausted before Christmas of his first year. He went home to stay, for his parents were poor. In those days there were no government or other educational loans. But when the family had gathered around the Christmas dinner table, his mother placed a fruit jar with coins and bills beside his plate and announced that Olin was indeed going back to school, after all. Looking at his mother's stained and coarsened hands, he began to realize that for many months she had cracked bushels and bushels of walnuts from the trees that grew on their place. By selling the kernels of the nuts, she had been able to save some money with which to send her son back to college. Olin Binkley resolved—as the enormousness of his mother's work and dedication became increasingly real to him while he looked from her walnut-stained hands to the contents of that jar—to put the kingdom of God first. He applied himself to his own work with a similar dedication, and before the age of twenty-five he earned a college degree, two seminary degrees, and a Ph.D. from Yale University. As a teacher of Christian ethics he influenced many students who became successful pastors, professors, and college presidents. Dr. Binkley became president of a seminary that trained hundreds of ministers under his leadership. The chapel of the campus of that flourishing seminary is named in his honor. He was the recipient of numerous honors and awards, but I believe I can truly say he never received any of them with a greater sense of gratitude and awe than he accepted that old glass jar presented by stained hands.

Your Part in the Social Order

The kingdom of God demands justice in the social order. As a nation, our priorities need to be rearranged. Full employment for every able-bodied person, an end to hunger and poverty, a national health insurance program, decent housing, excellence in public education, consumer rights, a safe environment, and peace are only a few of the items on the priority list.

When the kingdom of God is put first, all the things essential to life will be added. This is God's arithmetic. Jesus is talking to the emerging church when he commands, "Seek first the kingdom." The whole church as well as the individual member is to put the kingdom first. Only by doing so will you be free from anxiety about things.

Celebrating the Living Now

Finally, Jesus teaches that anxiety can be lived through by living today and celebrating the present moment. "Therefore do not be anxious about tomorrow, for tomorrow will be anxious for itself. Let the day's own trouble be sufficient for the day" (Matt. 6:34). Jesus appears to be saying that you should not be overly anxious about the things of tomorrow. Hence, you must acquire the art of living fully each day at a time. Deal only with today's trouble today. For, after all, you may not be alive tomorrow. Why worry for nothing, for a world that may not be your own? "Do not boast about tomorrow, for you do not know what a day may bring forth" (Prov. 27:1). The rich farmer (Luke 12:13–21) thought he had many goods laid up for many years. But he never lived to enjoy them.

Each day deserves your full involvement, attention, and active participation in the hopes, joys, and even pain that it brings.

Some people worry about the past and others about the future. Most of us are anxious about the present. As for the past, not much can be done to change it. You have to learn to live with it:

> The Moving Finger writes; and, having writ,
> Moves on: nor all your Piety nor Wit
> Shall lure it back to cancel half a Line,
> Nor all your Tears wash out a Word of it.
> (*The Rubáiyat of Omar Kháyyám*, LXXI;
> translated by Edward Fitzgerald)

Jesus has given the faithful believers assurance of his presence in the future. "Lo, I am with you always, to the close of the age" (Matt. 28:20). All you have is now. Moments become more precious as you get older. I must work, for the night is coming. At the age of seventy-two, I have exceeded the life expectancy of the average male born today in this country. Each hour, therefore, and each day, each additional month and year, must be filled with productive living. So you see why I cannot afford to lug tomorrow's troubles around today.

These are the basic principles that Jesus provides for coping with anxiety. We have not exhausted the supply, but these can help keep us from becoming overly anxious about things. My friend John Helm, whose grandfather was governor of Kentucky, inherited a large gold pocket watch from him. Since the watch was quite old and had not been in use for a long time, John took it to a skilled watchmaker. The watchmaker said that a certain part was missing and that he was unable to locate the needed part in antique watch supply houses. When John shared this information with me, I immediately contacted my brother, who is a watch specialist in another state. Sure enough, I soon received the missing part with a note attached, stating that it was not essential for the watch to run. Instead, the purpose of this part—a tiny collar for the stem—was to prevent the watch from being wound up too tight! So John's watch was repaired, returned to running condition, and it cannot be wound too tightly as long as the collar remains in place.

Jesus' teachings on anxiety do not remove all our anxieties. But they keep us from becoming too anxious, too tense, too uptight about things. You cannot attain full personhood if you are afflicted with overanxiousness. Commitment to Christ in a trustful, obedient relationship removes the roadblocks to wholeness. Community in a fellowship of faith provides a support system of sharing. It affords a sense of belonging and reduces the sense of anxiety characteristic of a tumbleweed existence. The comfort (or strengthening) of the Holy Spirit brings a recovery of wholeness. The Spirit strengthens you for the creative use of the gift of anxiety. You can live through anxiety if you "cast all your anxieties on him, for he cares about you" (I Peter 5:7).

The Anchoring of Your Anxiety

The author of the book of Hebrews declares that the Christian has hope as "a sure and steadfast anchor of the soul" (Heb. 6:19). The word translated "sure" *(asphalēs)* means firm, secure, safe, certain. The anchor of hope will hold firm, will not slip or lose its grip. It reaches into the Holy of Holies to Jesus Christ our High Priest. If you ever visit Mammoth Cave in Kentucky, you will hear about spelunkers, or cave explorers. Before entering a cave to explore it, spelunkers tie one end of a rope to an object outside the cave. Then, as they grope their way through the maze of passageways in the caverns, they unwind this rope. When they have finished exploring, they retrace their route to safety and survival by means of this guideline.

As a Christian you need to be tied, anchored to something beyond yourself. Otherwise, you will continue to be an anxious drifter. God is the rock to which the believer is anchored. Then without fear you can exclaim with the ancients, "Lord, thou hast been our dwelling place in all generations" (Ps. 90:1), and, "The eternal God is your dwelling place, and underneath are the everlasting arms" (Deut. 33:27).

Concern: A Godly Anxiety

Anxiety in the Bible has two meanings: unproductive fretfulness about things and productive concern for people and great causes. Wayne Oates calls the latter "godly anxiety." Paul gave expression to this sort of anxiety when he urged that church members avoid divisions and clashes but have "care for one another" (I Cor. 12:25). Paul's word for being concerned about others and caring for them *(merimnaō)* is the very word used by Jesus for being anxious about things (Matt. 6:25–34). Paul uses it here in a positive and productive sense. He personifies the parts of the human body as if each one is anxious for all the others. Modern science supports this view, for it has found that the billions of cells in the body are working together for the welfare of the whole.

Paul had a genuine anxiety for Timothy and his ministry. In commending this young minister to the Philippian church,

Paul declares, "I have no one like him, who will be genu-
inely anxious for your welfare" (Phil. 2:20). Paul's care for
all the churches of his day is expressed in godly anxiety for
their health and growth. He remarks, "There is the daily
pressure upon me of my anxiety for all the churches" (II Cor.
11:28).

More modern examples of godly anxiety or concern are
plentiful. You can think of many in your own experience. Let
me cite two for you here.

A small church in North Carolina was located near a
World War II army base, and occasionally servicemen visited there on Sundays. One Sunday, after the service, a
young enlisted man asked the pastor if he would perform a
marriage ceremony later in the week when his fiancée ar-
rived from New York State. Since the serviceman was a
stranger to the area, brought there by the circumstances of
his military assignment, he knew no local ministers but had
sensed a warmth in the morning service, which led him to
ask. The minister agreed to meet with the couple, counsel
them, and then perform the ceremony. He later expressed
his concern to the church member who arranged for flowers
for church services, for he felt there should be some sort of
tasteful floral arrangement for the little ceremony.

"Why, we can't let this young couple so far away from their
homes have a *lonely* wedding!" exclaimed the concerned
church member, and she enlisted several ladies of the church
to help. Thus the serviceman and his bride were surprised
and radiant when, on the day of their wedding, they marched
down the aisle to organ music provided by a volunteer or-
ganist. Flowers and candles were beautifully arranged in the
small church, and several pews were filled with strangers
(church members) who were concerned that their wedding
not be lonely. There was a reception afterward in the church
hall, with a simple punch and homemade cakes. With tearful
smiles of genuine gratitude, the young couple assured those

church members that the wedding ceremony was all the more unforgettable because of their caring concern.

We have looked at what anxiety is, its forms and its sources. The good news is that Jesus recognized and knew anxiety, but he overcame it. And we can deal with it, too, and direct it to more positive, creative purposes. You may have said at some time, "I'm going to pieces," or, "I'm afraid I'm coming apart." Anxiety is frequently the cause. I hope that the suggestions in this chapter can guide you, with God's help, to put the pieces back together.

Chapter 5

"I Don't Trust
Like I Did"

A minister (we will call him Don) sought my counsel. Don had just completed his doctor of philosophy degree at a nearby seminary. I asked him what the immediate issue was that impelled him to see me. He blurted out the words, "I don't trust like I did. I want to leave this place with a positive attitude, but I can't." Don was bitter because an administrator had several years before forced one of his best friends to leave that school. The offense had been marching and carrying a poster in a campus demonstration protesting the Vietnam war. This friend was able to complete his degree at another seminary. Don could not forgive and forget in this instance. He said he no longer trusted that administration. I suggested to Don that he was letting an official of the seminary control his emotional and mental life. He was letting it handicap his ministry. The anger was poisoning and destroying him. Then I added that administrators don't last forever, but that the institution would be there long after all involved were gone.

This man was presenting a concern that tears people apart: the collapse of trust. You too may be bothered with the plague of distrust.

What is trust? Simply put, trust is believing or having confidence in the integrity, honesty, reliability, and capability of a person or persons and institutions to perform as you expect them to. Doctors trust the stethoscope to provide them with accurate knowledge about the condition of a patient's heart. Parents trust the baby-sitter to take good care of their children. Although we trust people, they sometimes let us down. They disillusion us. They disappoint us. As the gospel song puts it, "The arm of flesh will fail you, you dare not trust your own."

Of course, all such trust is relative or limited. At the age of twelve, my daughter, Martha, made a hobby of inscribing rocks with calligraphy. When I admired her painted rocks, she promised to do a special one for me. I was pleased when she brought me a rock bearing the inscription *Love and Trust.* Martha said, "Turn the rock over and you will find your philosophy of life." When I read the other side I felt a bit uncomfortable, for I read, *Fully love everyone, but fully trust no one.* Reluctantly, I had to admit that she had captured my cautious attitude. While ideally and idealistically I *wanted* to love and trust everyone fully, my attitude was shaped partially by my years of living in ghettoes. Now that I live in a somewhat more affluent area, my home has been burglarized more than once. So the rock inscribed with my philosophy is still kept on my desk.

Perhaps this is where most of us are on the trust spectrum: "Trust everybody, but cut the cards yourself." "Trust God, but keep your powder dry." The slogan of the youth of the 1960s was "Never trust anyone over thirty." Now that they have grown older, some of them are saying, "Never trust anyone *under* thirty." Inscribed on our money is the motto "In God we trust." Yet you and I are tempted to trust the money rather than God.

The Crisis of Confidence in Institutions

For the past twenty-five years, Americans have joined in a louder and louder litany of distrust of our institutions and their leaders. The musical play *Camelot* is about King Arthur's court and the Round Table, where heroes with honor and integrity were believed and embraced by their fol-

lowers; they were trusted. But the litany I am about to re-
cite for you says that life in America today is no Camelot.
We have been through what President Carter called a "crisis
of confidence." We have been through many such crises.
This litany rehearses some of them. After you have read it, I
will ask you a question.

A Litany of Distrust

Recent surveys have drawn attention to a "collapsing-trust
syndrome." This refers to the way Americans tend to view
both their leaders and their national institutions. Among pro-
fessions once held in high esteem but now less trusted are
higher education, medicine, and the military. Organized religion, large corporations, and the White House rank among
the lowest on the trust rating scale (*Psychology Today,* Vol. 14,
No. 5, Oct. 1980, pp. 32ff.).

First, one of the many causes of the decline of national
trust was the Vietnam war. It is still a major contributing factor. The public learned that it was not told the whole truth
about the situation there. When we asked about the purposes and goals of our policies, and about the fighting conditions faced by our military forces, we got political responses rather than facts. We were told that everything was
under control, that "peace is at hand." Then came the Tet of-
fensive, in which over three hundred cities and towns were
attacked by the Vietcong. Evidence of the deception of
American citizens came from the Pentagon papers. These
were secret documents dealing with U.S. military operations
in Vietnam. The information was provided to *The New York
Times* by Daniel Ellsberg and published in 1971. It con-
firmed that American citizens were not being told the whole
truth.

Second, there was the revelation of illegal activities car-
ried on in connection with the 1972 presidential campaign.
The Watergate scandal took its toll of the trust capacity of
Americans. For the first time in history, a president of the

United States was forced to resign because of corruption in the White House.

Third, people living around the Three Mile Island electric power generating station near Harrisburg, Pennsylvania, trusted the government officials and industry executives when told by them that nuclear power plants were safe. With the 1979 accident at the Pennsylvania plant, their trust, and that of many other people around the country, was shattered.

Fourth, there came the Abscam project. In 1980 several FBI undercover agents offered bribes to congressmen. Some of these bribes were accepted. As a result, several congressmen went to prison.

Fifth, after an investigation of charges made in 1982, two congressmen were censured by the House of Representatives for having sexual relations with teenage congressional pages.

Sixth, the mass communications media have made a generous contribution to the erosion of trust in this country. Especially, there is growing skepticism and cynicism in response to false and misleading advertising. Even young children five or six years old can identify many misleading commercials.

Seventh, and finally, consider how organized religion has contributed to the lessening of our trust. Was the Jonestown mass suicide beyond your understanding? Could a so-called preacher really become demonic? How do you feel about the pitch for money made by religious groups on television? Have you noticed that many of the "religious shows" are just that—carefully staged "spectaculars" with all the props and cue cards that make for slick show business but offer little basis for faith or trust? The hokey claims of healing through shouts of "Praise the Lord!" and "Hallelujah!" cause many people to look at organized religion as a put-on. Many individuals have felt the shattering effects of a family member's becoming involved with supposedly religious cults. Churches are seeking ways to prevent their members' losing trust in their usual ways of doing things.

My apprehension is that by the time you read these words you will have added other items through listening to the morning and evening news.

Your Personal Responses

I want to ask you a question: Now that you have read this litany, what kinds of emotions does it generate in you? What are your personal responses to the events that have brought about a national decline of trust in institutions? Let me hazard some educated guesses.

One of your responses may be outrage, a sort of "how could they do this to me" attitude. You may use words like "incompetent," "no-good," "rascals," "con artists." In fact, you may have a difficult time finding words to express your outrage!

Another reaction may be a sort of hand-wringing helplessness. You may say to someone: "Isn't it awful? But there's nothing *we* can do about it." You shake your head in dismay, let out a heavy sigh, and shrug. The helpless feeling is almost overwhelming. It certainly throws your "power train" out of gear. You can race your engine, but it gets you nowhere.

Yet another emotional response may be avoidance, which builds on that helpless attitude. You may say, "I can't do anything about it, so I'll steer clear of it." Therefore you fail to register to vote. You don't bother to go to the polls on election day because you think your vote is not important. You just drop out of any involvement.

Then again, you may wallow in the suspicion and distrust, perhaps talking about "how rotten they are" and spreading your cloud of dismay and gloom to others.

Or you may respond with paranoia, which is a feeling that you are being persecuted. You distrust others and regard everyone as your enemy. The bureaucratic establishment becomes your archenemy. To cope with this alleged enemy, you may decide to get involved in the kind of group paranoia that exists in organizations such as the Ku Klux Klan or the Comitatus, groups outside the mainstream of our society.

The next step in your response could be violence, the drive to destroy the enemy. Now you have reached the destructive end of the whole negative emotional response to the problem of distrust of the institutions of our organized life together.

There are many causes for our lack of trust in our institutions. And there are many possible responses. *Yet we continue to use the institutions.* (This indicates that we trust them more than we may think.) The will to trust is strong. That is the point of the *Peanuts* cartoon strip that appears every fall, in which poor gullible Charlie Brown tries to placekick a football and always lands on his face (or back) because Lucy jerks the ball away at the last moment. What Lucy claims to be trying to teach Charlie is not to be too trusting. But he keeps on trying to kick the football year after year. Why? Charlie Brown explains that it is due to his "undying faith in human nature."

Isn't it amazing how trustful you really are? You place your life in the hands of the doctor and the pharmacist. Every time you get on a plane and fly you trust the pilot and crew and the builders of the plane. You trust the makers of your car, of the elevator, of the bridge, and of public transportation vehicles. Trust is one of the most remarkable traits you have. You find trust absolutely essential in every area of your life. Most organized life would come to a halt and end in chaos without trust. Even a criminal gang has to maintain some degree of trust among its members.

Alternatives to Futility

Trust is both a personal and a social good. It has to be protected and promoted—as Sissela Bok declares—just as much as the air we breathe and the water we drink. Why? Because when trust is damaged, the whole community suffers. And when it is destroyed, there is chaos and collapse (*Lying: Moral Choice in Public and Private Life,* pp. 26–27). To close the credibility gap, positive steps need to be taken to promote trust.

Let me suggest some things you can do to rebuild your trust in institutions, because trust is both a social and a personal necessity.

First, trust begins in the home, the primary institution. Notice that the litany of distrust does not mention the home. The will to trust comes from the home—yours and mine. Long before you had any inkling of institutions, politics, nuclear disasters, and war you formed attitudes of trust or distrust toward life.

Erik Erikson, the distinguished psychiatrist, describes eight stages of ego development, or self-development, from birth to death. In the first stage, the infant learns to trust. This is called the oral or sensory stage. It covers the earliest years of your life. During this infant stage, you learned whether you could trust the world about you or whether your dominant feeling must be distrust. Depending on the mother-child relationship, the baby develops a basic feeling of trust that his or her wants will be regularly satisfied by this wonderful, caring adult.

Erikson observes that during the second six months the child's teeth erupt painfully. So now the baby's dominant behavior moves toward biting, which itself is a movement of "taking" as opposed to merely being a passive receiver. There is also a shadow of sadness and homesickness for the warmth and security of the earlier relationship when weaning takes place. Eden was lost! But the child survives both weaning and teething and, if basic trust is strong, he or she will have a built-in hope for a healthy development in other stages of life.

It should be noted that the basic problem of trust-distrust is not resolved once and for all during the first year of life, for it arises at every successive stage of development. For example, if as a child you entered the first grade with an attitude of distrust, you may in time have developed a relationship of trust with a teacher who showed that he or she was trustworthy. Thus the early distrust was overcome. Then again, the teacher may have been untrustworthy, thereby confirming your suspicions of the world. Likewise, any child who has a sense of trust can have a sense of distrust activated at a later stage in life. For example, a child's parents may be divorced under bitter and unhappy circumstances. This can cause buried distrust to surface again in the youngster.

So the place to start building trust is in the home, especially during the first year of the life of children you have and know. Mothers are of primary importance here, since children usually receive first impressions from them.

The second step in building trust is to think and read. Don't just stew in the juice of your outrage. Be willing to read articles and books that you know you may disagree with. Be willing to look at another person's point of view. Take the responsibility of forming your own ideas and opinions, based on the best information you can find.

Third, do something. You are not as helpless as you may think. For example, we are seeing increasingly that voters are getting their messages across to the politicians. Recently a Republican from Arkansas made a speech on the floor of the House of Representatives. Referring to the civil rights struggles in his state in the 1960s, he asked, "Do you know what we learned out of all that? That the great changes are not made here in the legislative chambers or in the judicial halls. The great changes in this world are made in the hearts and minds of men and women." As you will recall, the voters in California had a grass-roots tax revolt and voted for Proposition 13. In my own local community, voters have resoundingly defeated increased taxes for schools, and they have twice organized to defeat the merger of the city and county governments. These voters are trying to tell the leadership something, and the leaders are listening.

Fourth, stay where the action is. Get involved. The story is told of the schoolteacher who, while sitting at her desk when her students were outside for recess, was surprised when one lad rushed in breathlessly from the playground. "Here, Teacher!" he exclaimed as he pressed an object into her palm. "Hold my glass eye while I go out yonder and fight!" He rushed out as hurriedly as he had entered and plunged headlong into the fray. Instead of withdrawing and avoiding involvement, make up your mind, based on your own beliefs and information; then register, vote, express your ideas, act on your convictions. Don't leave it to someone else, or you may end up merely "holding their glass eye" while they get involved.

Fifth, deal with leaders directly, not through whispering campaigns of distrust. Matthew 18:15 says, "If your brother sins against you, go and tell him his fault, between you and him alone. If he listens to you, you have gained your brother." Remember that elected officials and leaders in places of responsibility are answerable to those who have put them there. You have every right to deal with leaders directly. Write them. Go to see them.

Sixth, test your own rhetoric, your talk, for its paranoia. Apply a test to determine if you are reporting the facts or merely your feelings or the biases of others. Noted sociologist R. H. Giddings suggests the following: "I want to believe that it is, but then, *is it,* always or generally? Does anybody *know* that it usually is, or is everybody just *saying* that it is?" ("The Scientific Scrutiny of Societal Facts" in *The Making of Society;* The Modern History, 1937). So before you relate an incident, check it out. Remember that your actions should be undergirded or backed up with facts.

Trust in Interpersonal Relations

Some studies show that people who tend to have trust are neither more gullible nor less intelligent than those who do not. Julian Rotter, a clinical psychologist at the University of

Connecticut, developed an Interpersonal Trust Scale (ITS) consisting of twenty-five statements that people can rate on a 5-point scale ranging from "strongly agree" to "strongly disagree." Those respondents who score in the top 50 percent are called "high trusters," while those whose scores fall in the lower half are "low trusters."

Rotter defines trust as a person's belief that individuals as well as groups will behave in accordance with their promises ("Trust Everybody, but Cut the Cards," *Psychology Today,* Vol. 14, No. 5, Oct. 1980, p. 32). Some fifteen thousand people, mostly students, have been surveyed since 1966. The results are worth noting. High trusters are themselves more trustworthy, better adjusted, and more likable. Moreover, they are frequently involved in beneficial social efforts like scouting and other volunteer work ("Trust and Gullibility," ibid., pp. 35–42, 102). Yet it appears that trust is declining among persons in our culture. Years ago the maxim "An honest man's word is as good as his bond" was generally accepted. At the present time, it is advisable to get everything in writing and keep copies, even in dealing with religious folk.

Trusting Friends

Your friendships are built on trust. Betrayal of trust by your friend may have been one of your most painful experiences. The psalmist becomes a victim of betrayal by an intimate or close friend.

> It is not an enemy who taunts me—
>   then I could bear it;
> it is not an adversary who deals
>   insolently with me—
>   then I could hide from him.
> But it is you, my equal,
>   my companion, my familiar friend.
> We used to hold sweet converse together;
>   within God's house we walked in fellowship.
>   (Ps. 55:12–14)

Here were friends who shared intimate thoughts and counsel. They walked in harmony and with a sense of purpose.
But one violated their covenant. He concealed his actions
with deceit and double-dealing:

> His speech was smoother than butter,
>   yet war was in his heart;
> his words were softer than oil,
>   yet they were drawn swords.
>   (Ps. 55:21)

Trust in Marriage

If you are married, your spouse should be your dearest
friend. Broken trust is extremely destructive at this level of
interpersonal relations. High trust is both expected and essential for a successful marriage. As a pastoral counselor I
have had numerous cases of broken trust and shaken marriages. Take a typical triangle situation, for example. The
husband is sexually involved with his secretary when he is
supposed to be out of town on business. His wife discovers
this and says she can never trust him again. He has broken
their covenant of trust. He has his work ahead of him to re-
assure her and to rebuild that trust. She is being tested to
trust him enough to give him the chance to rebuild.

Building trust among persons is the basis for productive
living in wider areas of interpersonal relations. Such trust is
built by consistent covenant keeping. Keeping promises to
your friends is a way to a trustful relationship. Faithfulness
in marriage is basic to a trustful relationship. You yourself
can develop trust by being open and aboveboard in all your
relationships. At the same time, remember that it takes time
for trust to develop. More than time, it takes courage and
greatness of heart.

Developing Trust in Government

Trust in authority figures has declined all over the world, particularly in the developed countries (Richard Sennett, *Authority*; Alfred A. Knopf, 1980). Yet a considerable residue of trust in American government remains, for ours is generally a trusting society. But the nontrusters are among us. When we were asked to drive less in order to conserve gasoline during the recent oil shortage, nontrusters thought the whole deal was a rip-off of some kind and that there was really plenty of gasoline but it was being held back to increase the profits of the oil companies. Nevertheless, the American people have changed their driving habits, and the oil industry—even OPEC—has taken notice.

A Sense of Vocation

As an alternative to futility, have a sense of your vocation to be a part of your government, and don't let anyone disenfranchise you. In order to develop more trust both in government and in interpersonal relations, several positive actions will be necessary.

First, you and I will need a clear sense of personal calling. Political responsibility is a vital part of our Christian calling or vocation. Paul the apostle says, "Only let your manner of life be worthy of the gospel of Christ" (Phil. 1:27). The Greek verb *politeuomai* literally refers to exercising citizenship and the passage really says, "Let your citizenship or political actions be in keeping with the gospel of Christ." This means we are to act responsibly in the political process of the community. But too often—like Moses, who was called to liberate his fellow Israelites from Egyptian bondage—we tend to put up all sorts of excuses to avoid doing our political duty.

You and I are responsible for choosing political leaders of integrity. We are to set a good example of citizenship by becoming informed about political issues, registering, voting, and praying for public officials that they may function with honor and fairness to all citizens.

Second, our nation must recover its sense of vocation. When a country loses its sense of mission, it is headed for the rubbish heap of history. God called Israel to a specific mission in the world. That mission is summed up by the prophet Isaiah:

> I am the LORD, I have called you in righteous-
>   ness,
> I have taken you by the hand and kept you;
> I have given you as a covenant to the people,
>   a light to the nations,
>   to open the eyes that are blind,
> to bring out the prisoners from the dungeon,
>   from the prison those who sit in darkness.
>   (Isa. 42:6–7)

Israel failed to fulfill its mission in the world and God raised up another people for this purpose (I Peter 2:9).

America's sense of vocation and goals is ambiguous. At one time, many said America's purpose was to bring about the kingdom of God on earth. But this goal became secularized and was identified with social progress and with political programs such as the New Deal and the Great Society. Now only confusion and contradictions exist about America's mission in the world. Recovery of clear-cut goals for our existence as a nation is essential to survival.

Self-Criticism

An important step in developing trust is the capacity for self-criticism. Do you think your distrust of government justifies your being dishonest? Are you scrupulous in reporting all your income on the tax forms? Are you aware of the little ways you bend the laws, at the same time justifying your actions by insisting that "everyone else does the same thing" or "the big guys get by with it, so I can too"?

Beyond this personal level, if trust in our government is

to increase, we will have to begin by dealing with our sins. This will not be easy, for the Pharisee syndrome is likely to prevail. Business will blame labor for failures, and labor will accuse business of not sharing the profits. It will be difficult for both groups to be self-critical. The same is true in political and interracial relations.

On the national level, too, we must be able to exercise self-criticism. One of the conditions that the government of Iran sought to enforce for the release of the American hostages in 1980 was that the United States confess to wrongdoing, to sin against Iran. But how does a nation confess collective guilt? Some evangelists are fond of quoting II Chronicles 7:14 as the answer to this problem:

> If my people who are called by name humble themselves, and pray and seek my face, and turn from their wicked ways, then I will hear from heaven, and will forgive their sin and heal their land.

In our diverse society with its many religious groups, this teaching could well be applied and could lead to the restoration of respect and the rekindling of trust and confidence in our nation's leaders. God's people living out the ethical teaching of Scripture can restore faith and trust.

It is easy for our leaders to say that the Soviet Union is "the focus of evil" and yet to overlook our own evil ways. The United States is guilty to some degree of the same sins we condemn in other countries. If justice is "for all," as the Pledge of Allegiance says, then humility is in order as a major corrective to the distortions of judgment we as a nation have about ourselves and others. In the light of justice and humility, no state or social system is above criticism. This includes both communist and capitalist countries.

The Renewal of Statesmanship

We must somehow elect statesmen rather than politicians to public office before a climate of trust can be developed in our nation. A statesman is a political leader who demonstrates wisdom, sensitivity to the needs of constituents, and insight in promoting the public good. A politician usually doesn't enjoy a notable reputation. He or she is seen as seeking public office for private gain. Will Rogers used to say on the radio, "Honesty is not an issue in politics; it is a miracle!" Politicians promise more than they can deliver. They promise to bring the voters a better life without their needing to become better people. At the present time, trust in politicians is perhaps at its lowest level in our history as a nation.

Statesmen, by contrast, are a rare breed. They are elected to serve the people and the nation, and they do just that. Abraham Lincoln was a great statesman. A humble man, he resisted the temptation to say that God was on his side in the Civil War. In his second inaugural address (perhaps the most profoundly theological statement in American political literature), Lincoln wrestled with the knowledge that people on both sides of the conflict prayed to the same God and read the same Bible. Neither could be entirely right. The war was nearly over. At the end of his typically short address, Lincoln made a plea for achieving a just and lasting peace "with malice toward none, with charity for all." He seemed to have no desire for revenge or to punish the enemies of the Union. In this, Lincoln bore witness to God's love and forgiveness.

Statesmen are rare, but I am fortunate to have known a few in my time, and they have kept alive my trust in the political system.

Leadership Versus Domination

A leader is one who has persuasive qualities and whose adherents freely follow. Leadership is the activity of influencing people to work toward some desirable, worthwhile goal. Leadership can be exercised on the basis of authority or power attached to an office that requires respect and obedience. Real leadership is power *with* people, while authority is power *over* people. So genuine leadership is the persuasive power that comes from personality apart from an office.

Leaders should put their feet in the right way and stand firm. There are few leaders who do this, because it is costly. I once heard a series of lectures by the great Christian leader John R. Mott, in which he observed the prices one must pay to be an effective leader. Among these are thoroughness, rigorous study, intensity, steadfastness, energy, service, self-denial, and loneliness. (See *Leadership Demanded for This Momentous Time,* pp. 14–20; reprint, Stetson University Press, 1974.) I would add that the leader chooses to deal with people in terms of human life values and not in terms of bureaucratic self-maintenance.

A Sense of Justice

Trust has diminished in our society because of injustice— political, economic, and social. For trust to increase, justice must become more widespread. We must obey the command of God to "let justice roll down like waters, and righteousness like an ever-flowing stream" (Amos 5:24). For the ancient Greeks, justice was giving each person his or her due. In the Bible, justice is practically equated with righteousness.

Justice is fair play, in modern terms. John Rawls of Harvard has a point of view about justice that is close to the Golden Rule in the Bible. In making decisions, moral and social, ask yourself what you would feel about a proposed policy if you were to be one of the persons affected by your decision (*A Theory of Justice*; Harvard University Press, 1971). This means, of course, that you put yourself in the other person's shoes.

Empathy is the generator both of justice and of personal confidence and trust. The promotion of this sort of justice in the courts, in government, in human relations, and in your personal life is your duty and that of every citizen. Only as justice increases in society will trust grow.

Love and justice are inseparable. I recall that in my home

church, before the civil rights movement, we used to sing with gusto about the "Old Time Religion" that "makes me love everybody." But "everybody" was not specific. It meant we loved those who didn't bother us, who were just like us and didn't make us uncomfortable in our prejudices. Justice, on the other hand, is love's specific instrument; it gives direction and concreteness to love.

The Shaking of the Foundations

In Hebrews 12:27, the writer talks about the "removal of what is shaken, as of what has been made, in order that what cannot be shaken may remain." The minister who said, "I don't trust like I did," had been shaken. What could be shaken had to be removed. The litany of distrust in our institutions that we recited represents *how* what can be shaken is being removed. The foundations of our national and personal order are being shaken. Yet the things that cannot be shaken will remain. What are some of those things? In them your trust can rise above your personal heritage and the sorry scheme of things that we have surveyed in this chapter. If your ideals have been illusions and you are disillusioned, now you are prepared to see and hear, not shadows and echoes of the eternal God's trustworthiness but God's own light and God's own truth. In this sense, God is redeeming your life from the idolatry of political groupings of power, churchly towers of Babel, and your own personal delusion that, if you had all power, things would be perfect.

When my daughter presented me with the stone on which was inscribed what she thought was my philosophy of life, "Fully love everyone, but fully trust no one," I felt a bit uneasy. It seemed incomplete. So when I later had that motto put on a bookmark, I made an addition. Now it reads, "Fully love everyone, but fully trust no one—except God."

Chapter 6

"Is My Life Over?"

A song made popular by singer Peggy Lee several years ago had the title, "Is That All There Is?" The lyrics were questioning the things one can see, hear, and feel, as well as emotions. Concrete objects are indeed real but temporal. There is more.

If you take the Bible seriously, this life is not all there is. Yet many with shattering experiences in their lives find it difficult to believe this. Bad things happen, and you are likely to ask, "Is my life over?"

Not Over Yet

From among the thousands of students I have taught during the last forty years, James Bouchillon stands out vividly in my memory. Jim, as he liked to be called, received his college degree and came to Southern Baptist Theological Seminary. After earning a seminary degree, he started graduate studies. One day early in the course of this work, he staggered into my office. I was startled at his lack of coordination and helped him to a chair, where he related a tragic story. Doctors had just informed him that he had multiple sclerosis. In the light of this bad news, he was uncomplaining. Rather, he declared that from the time he was a little boy he wanted to be a preacher. Now that his ministerial career was to be cut short, he planned to return to Alabama for the remainder of his life. "Several small country churches near my home," he declared, "cannot afford a pastor. I am going to preach in them as long as I am able to do so." He did just that. His life was not over yet.

Living on the Edge

You will recall the wonderful true story of Helen Keller, who as a nineteen-month-old child was stricken with blindness and deafness. Some people are unaware that Anne Sullivan, the remarkable teacher who helped young Helen learn language communication, was herself visually handicapped and had spent her early years enmeshed in the miseries of a squalid poorhouse. Through disciplined determination and intellectual effort, both were able to overcome heavy odds and achieve the nearly impossible.

In another instance, John Howard Griffin, noted author of *Black Like Me* and other important works and an unusually talented, courageous man, spent most of his final days as a near-invalid. In his last letter to me before his death in 1980, he wrote: "Half of the heart has died, so the rest of me struggles to keep me at least half alive. It is an enormously clarifying thing to live on the edge of the precipice."

Many people feel they are living on that edge of the steep cliff. Others are sure they have already gone over the edge and are shattered. Some may have physical handicaps like those of the people mentioned above. For persons who are not born with such handicaps but rather acquire them later in life through an accident or illness, the event can be traumatic and disabling in an intense way. They have to deal with their rage against the fate that has "done this dreadful thing" to them. They may suffer depression resulting from the fear that the best of life will never be accessible to them, a longing for what used to be, a fear of rejection and of being a burden to those they love. They have to adjust to the stare of strangers and self-conscious overconcern of well-meaning people, as well as the attempt, by casual acquaintances, to avoid acknowledging the reality of their condition. Along with these and other emotions, the physically handicapped must learn to adjust to whatever mechanical assistance is available—wheelchairs, specially outfitted vehicles—as well as high curbs, heavy or narrow doors, and cumbersome equipment. They have to deal, too, with their own resentment of those who don't have to face such hardships day after day. They must cope not only with the inconvenience and pain but also with their sense of the injustice of it all.

The Perils of Retirement

He sat there before me, his head buried in his hands, depressed, hopeless. This was a man of sixty-seven years who had worked all his adult life but now was retired from his job as an assembly-line worker. Life for him had lost meaning because he felt useless. His wife had come into a substantial inheritance and now she was taking charge, making the decisions for them. At her insistence they had moved into an upper middle class community. Feeling keenly that he was out of place as well as out of the familiar routine of his work, the man was miserable. "I have thought of suicide," he admitted, "but I'm not sure I can go through with that." Medical tests had shown that he had no major illness, but he had lost interest in maintaining his health and even his life.

The changes brought on by retirement from the workplace seem to be traumatic for many people. My barber, who is something of a homespun philosopher, recently told me that several of his clients had died shortly after retirement at sixty-five. He concluded that this happened because they had nothing to do; they had no hobby, no meaningful work, no sense of making any significant contribution to the community. Retirement can be both destructive to your life and disruptive to your marriage. Whether you are a husband or a wife who has worked outside the home, you should develop interests of your own. Your spouse may not be able to stand having you around the house all the time. It need not be this way if you avoid overinvestment in one profession or job.

But if you have put all your eggs in one basket, you may find that life is over for you at retirement, and, like so many elderly persons, you will just be marking time. Developing skills in other areas may mean a chance to start a whole new career.

If you do not prepare for retirement by developing hobbies or skills for further work, you may imperil your health and even hasten your death. More about this later.

The Pain of Loss

One who has suffered loss by death knows that after the initial grief and shock there comes the difficult labor of picking up the pieces. Several weeks after the death of Dr. Duke McCall's wife, a gentleman came up to him and said, "I want you to know how sorry I am that you lost your wife."

"You don't understand," replied Dr. McCall. "My wife is not lost. I *know* where Marguerite is. *I* am the one who is now lost!"

At the time I began writing this book, news reports from Israel drew attention to Prime Minister Menachem Begin's increasing withdrawal from national leadership after the death of his invalid wife in 1982. At public functions and in the legislative hall he appeared to be listless, preoccupied, bored, and even just marking time. What was left in life for him now, at his age?

I can identify to a degree with Mr. Begin. Thirty years ago, my own beloved first wife died. She had not been ill for a long time. In fact, we had no indication that anything was seriously amiss in her pregnancy. Her death was sudden, totally unexpected. It left me in shock, confusion, numbness, and despair. Not only did I have to deal with my own anguish, I also had to interpret to my two young sons what had happened. They had thought, when we rushed their mother to the hospital, that she would return later with a new brother—or perhaps they might even accept a new sister! But instead, I returned alone, bringing them only sad and unbelievable news. The pattern of our lives—individually and together—was altered beyond comprehension. I will speak of this again.

Another kind of painful loss is that which comes with divorce. Despite recent statistics showing that, in the United States, for every two marriages there is one divorce, the breakup of a marriage still is usually a shattering, miserable time of turmoil. The sense of failure is magnified by a complex mixture of feelings of anger and hurt, revenge-seeking, and self-justification. The feeling of rejection and the loss of a sense of self-worth are devastating. These problems are compounded if children are involved; such long-term difficulties have no quick and easy solutions. Often the children are used as pawns in the parents' struggles. They suffer from torn loyalties and stresses that often get in the way of wholesome adjustments in school or social situations. Establishing new life patterns is never easy, even for those who may feel relieved in getting out of a miserable marriage.

Facing such day-to-day difficulties seems more than some people can handle. They seek escape—whether by actual flight from the scene or through drugs and alcohol, involvement in sexual affairs, or descent into deep depression often requiring hospitalization. For them, life as it once was appears to be over. Certainly it is altered. For a few persons, the intensity of attention and concern received from family and friends after a loss by death or divorce can become a heady experience they don't wish to relinquish. They secretly relish having others lavish sympathy on them and make decisions for them. Therefore they resist moving beyond the abyss of grief to more productive living.

Being Unemployed

In these days of high unemployment it is not difficult to find persons whose lives have been disrupted by the loss of a job. Often the job has been a major factor in their picture of who they actually are. The work they have performed has been important in determining their self-image and also society's view of who they are. The sudden and unwanted separation from that self-defining work—to say nothing of the financial burden—can activate some of the same emotions of anger, frustration, confusion, helplessness, and hopelessness generated by the losses mentioned earlier. The strain on family relationships is tremendous. And the feeling of worthlessness is increased by the degrading experience of returning again and again to the unemployment office or waiting in long lines for food handouts. While you might think that being among so many others in the same condition would foster a sense of togetherness and friendly camaraderie, it seldom does. For much of the rest of society says glibly, "Oh, there's always work for those who *want* to work!" or "You can find a job if you try." Some decry the amount of money the government allots to the unemployed and the poverty-stricken. You may recall a recent experiment by Secretary of Agriculture John R. Block (a millionaire), who with his wife, his daughter, and a girlfriend of the daughter's, "lived for a week" on the maximum food-stamp allotment ($58) for a family of this size. There were numerous responses of dismay at the insensitivity involved in this kind of unrealistic promotional stunt. As one opinion-page letter writer put it, "The whole exercise ignores one of the most pertinent characteristics of poverty: the unrelenting hopelessness involved."

An article in *U.S. News & World Report* (June 14, 1982; pp. 81–82) is entitled "New Health Hazard: Being Out of Work." In this article a sociologist states that 4 percent more people are committed to prisons when the unemployment rate rises by just 1 percent. Moreover, there is a marked increase in murders, suicides, and mental-health-related admissions during periods of increasing unemployment. Similarly, there appears to be a correlation between joblessness and higher rates of stress-related illnesses such as cirrhosis of the liver and heart disease. Many mental-health clinics are linking job loss to increases in crime, child abuse, family upheaval, sleep disorders, and physical and mental problems. So these are society's problems. But the "pink-slip syndrome" is an intensely personal one, too. Added to the emotions mentioned earlier is the fear of poverty with its hopelessness.

An Identity Crisis

The importance of self-identity, and of its loss or assaults on it, can be seen in what frequently happens to young people when they leave home to go to college or serve in the armed forces or seek a job. Leaving the security of home is especially difficult for those who have left a warm, perhaps protective environment. Such self-defining limits are seldom present in the new environment. Bumping up against the reality of people with differing values and life-styles can be very unsettling and can cause many a young person to go through an identity crisis. He or she may begin to think, "I've really blown it now," after some experimentation and testing of long-held values. As a result of this struggle, such persons become prime targets for cult recruiters, or they may try to forget their "prodigal son" actions by burying themselves in alcohol or drug abuse. Are they now beyond hope? Have they moved so far away from their old life that, as Thomas Wolfe put it, they really "can't go home again"?

The Pit of Utter Despair

You may have had the experience of being shattered by a nervous or emotional breakdown. I talked with one such person recently, a woman who had attempted suicide. She said, "I know it's hard for others to realize, but when you're in that kind of condition you have absolutely no control over your thoughts, your actions, or your words. You are aware of a great deal, but you can't work it into any kind of reasonable pattern. Control is impossible—completely beyond you."

The noted theologian, writer, and preacher Harry Emerson Fosdick describes in his autobiography (*The Living of These Days,* pp. 71–75) his own battle with a breakdown when he was a seminary student: "It was the beginning of one of the most hideous experiences of my life. . . . One dreadful day I reached the pit of utter despair, sure all my hopes were vain and that I was finished." He seriously considered suicide.

Numerous other people, including Tolstoy, Mark Twain, and William James, also found themselves in the pit of despair, thinking about how to end their own lives. You probably know the names of people you can add to that list.

Making the Most of the Rest of Your Life

Neither you nor I know how long our own life will be. Many times—however long our life—we will have to pick up the pieces and move forward. A part of the humanity we share is that we fail and we suffer. As Paul expressed it in Romans 3:23, "All have sinned and fall short of the glory of God." But the good news is that in Christ you and I can reclaim our place within the glory of God. Let's look at how to refit the shattered pieces of our broken lives.

Avoiding Idolatry

First of all, recognize the danger in making an idol out of what you lost. As has been indicated, what you have lost may be physical ability or prowess, a loved one, a marriage relationship, self-identity, a job. But whatever the loss was, you are still *you*—a child of God created in his image. The object of loss was not the God worthy of your worship; don't elevate *it* to the position of a god, lest you engage in idolatry.

Recognize that the loss or the event causing you pain is not really the end of the world. In fact, you can make the pain work for you. That is what my friend Wayne Oates does. For many years he has been troubled with severe back pain. Surgery did not relieve it. While waiting in his hospital room for his return from the operating room, I noticed a writing pad on the bedside table. It contained the outline of a book he had begun to write just before the operation. The title was *The Revelation of God in Human Suffering.* During the recuperation period he completed the book, drawing on his own experiences. An elaborate set of personal disciplines—traction, exercise, rest, weight control, physiotherapy—help him to cope with continuing pain. But when the pain awakens him early in the morning, he writes books. By using his mind and hands with intensity and purpose, he can divert his own attention from the pain, as well as create something that may be helpful to others. He has written more than thirty books, edited dozens more, published numerous articles, and inspired many others to write. Besides writing, he travels all over the country lecturing, speaking, and counseling. And he maintains a full schedule of teaching and counseling at our local medical school.

Another surgical patient, Kentucky's governor John Y. Brown, said recently of the triple bypass heart surgery that almost claimed his life in June 1983, "It's sort of like being born again to me. I'm a great believer in life. Out of every crisis comes opportunity. Hopefully, something good will come out of this. I think it will change my life, and it needed to be changed." He pointed out that he was not smoking at all, had lost 25 pounds, was exercising faithfully, and was placing renewed emphasis on family relationships.

Recovering from the Loss of a Loved One

Even the crisis of losing a loved one need not be the end of your own vitality in life. Timothy George has preached a practical and moving sermon entitled simply "Doing the Next Thing." In this sermon he urges those of us in the throes of grief, confusion, and numbness to take the important first step to recovery by "doing the next thing that needs to be done, whether it be even so simple a step as brushing your teeth and combing your hair, putting a load of laundry into the washing machine, making up the bed." By the simple ritual of "doing the next thing," we are kept in touch with the rhythms of life and our vitality begins slowly to return. Let me give you some examples.

When their baby was six months old, a young mother received the dreaded telegram informing her that her soldier husband had been killed in action. He had never seen his baby boy. The anguished wife was almost immobilized with grief. As she expressed it later, "I didn't feel I could go on one step further, but I had to. The baby made me have to. I had to get up every day because the baby would cry, and he *needed* me." Gradually the young woman's vitality began to reappear through this care.

In another situation of loss, Eleanor Nutt tells poignantly of how, after the untimely death of her husband, renowned humorist Grady Nutt, her friend Dottie went with her to the supermarket. As they moved slowly through the brightly lit aisles, Dottie quietly told Eleanor—who in previous times had moved swiftly and decisively through these same aisles—what she needed to place in her shopping basket. Her friend was helping Eleanor to do the next thing.

In that step-by-step process of doing the next thing, reestablishing our pattern of life, you will be sometimes "surprised by joy," as C. S. Lewis says. In my own grief situation, after the death of my first wife, it was as I was able to reestablish my teaching routine that I met the woman I later married. She helped me and my two little boys feel like a complete family again. And later our union provided those sons with a delightful sister, then a "hero-worshiping" (of them) little brother. For me, Helen has provided "beauty for ashes, the oil of joy for mourning, the garment of praise for the spirit of heaviness" (Isa. 61:3). Thus, for twenty-seven years I have known the height of joy and fulfillment in the marriage relationship that can come only to those who have known the depth of despair.

Retirement or Retreading?

At my retirement dinner five years ago, several friends made the usual glowing speeches, which of course I greatly appreciated. But the most memorable one, I thought, was that given by Rev. J. V. Bottoms, beloved black pastor, who years before had been one of my students. "Brother Barnette," he intoned in that rich, full voice of his, "lots of people here tonight have given you advice. But the words I want to leave with you are these: Don't give up until you *go* up!"

When it was my turn to respond to all these speeches, I assured the group, "The word retirement is not in my vocabulary. You see, old professors of Christian ethics don't *retire;* they merely *retread* for the rest of the journey!" My "retread" job included joining the faculty of the local medical school as a clinical professor—and writing books.

You can retread too. Develop new hobbies. Read, or reread, some classics you neglected in school. Use your local library. Check out some community volunteer groups. Sponsor a tutoring program in your local schools. You might, with your spouse or a good friend, begin making lists of new activities and interests you can pursue for your retreading job. Then follow through on it.

Handicapped—But Not Hopeless

Michael Godwin is a twenty-year-old Kentuckian who was born with cerebral palsy. He was placed in Hazelwood, a facility for the mentally retarded. The staff and Michael's family believed that his mind was as hopelessly crippled as his body; they were wrong. His was a perfectly good mind trapped inside a handicapped body. As the reporter who told Michael's story said, "He lived in a one-way world, understanding what was said to him but unable to reply." His life didn't change until he was fifteen and a new teacher at the facility spotted "a light in his eyes that made him different from the others." She taught him to communicate by a complicated tray (a lapboard) with about 300 words, phrases, numbers, and letters. When a questioner moves a finger across the board, Michael can nod when the word he wants to say is reached. Another teacher at Hazelwood speaks with awe of the change that took place when Michael learned to communicate. "It was like giving him wings," she said. Those who have come to know this young man now say that he is a person of intelligence, compassion, and gentle humor. He gives his own story in a letter composed with the word tray and a questioner:

> I'm happy I'm out of Hazelwood. I have friends who come over to my apartment. I was not happy at Hazelwood. I was not dumb but they thought I was at first. People would pass me by in the halls and say things not knowing that I understood— but I did. It took them a long time to find out— too long. I wish I had started school sooner (I started at fifteen). Don't stop because you are in a wheelchair.

Out of the Pit

The woman whom I quoted earlier, who suffered an emotional breakdown and then attempted suicide, explains her action: "My suicide attempt was a cry for help." Having received good professional care, she recovered and now holds a highly responsible job and is functioning well. She no longer lives in the pit of despair.

Harry Emerson Fosdick, whose breakdown in seminary we have mentioned, was able to use his pit experience as a chance to learn and grow. He wrote:

> This whole horrid experience was one of the most important factors in my preparation for the ministry. For the first time in my life I faced, at my wit's end, a situation too much for me to handle. I went down into the depths where self-confidence becomes ludicrous. . . . I, who had thought myself strong, found myself beaten, unable to cope not only with outward circumstances but even with myself. In that experience I learned some things about religion that theological seminaries do not teach. I learned to pray, not because I had adequately argued out prayer's rationality, but because I desperately needed help from a Power greater than my own. I learned that God, much more than a theological proposition, is an

immediately available Resource; that just as around our bodies is a physical universe from which we draw all our physical energy, so around our spirits is a spiritual Presence in living communion with whom we can find sustaining strength. Without that experience I do not think I would have written one of my early books, *The Meaning of Prayer.* And I learned as well much about human nature that academic courses in psychology leave out. (*The Living of These Days,* p. 75)

Things We Can Do

What if the new teacher at Hazelwood had ignored the light in Michael's eyes or felt the word tray was too complicated to work out? Suppose Dottie had not helped Eleanor make those simple selections at the supermarket? Suppose Harry Emerson Fosdick had not received medical care and support? No doubt you can think of individuals who have provided a kind of support system in your own time of brokenness. Perhaps you have been the key support figure for someone in need. The fact that you have been or are unemployed just now may mean that you are precisely the one who can give encouragement to another person in the same situation, or that you may be able to give advice or help to agencies trying to meet the needs of the unemployed. Through your own suffering and brokenness you may have far more effectiveness than you ever thought possible. Just as our fellowship in the human condition means we have all sinned and fall short of the glory of God, even so we can help support each other in striving for wholeness.

Really Good News

In order to pick up the pieces of our own shattered lives, you and I need to ask God to grant us sensitivity and perception to see a new design, a "newness of life" pattern that can shape us. He gives us this newness of life in Christ Je-

sus. We are not to ignore our woundedness, our brokenness. But we can affirm our shatteredness because, even as
your own knowledge of suffering has enabled you to help
others, Christ himself has suffered for and with us. And he
wants to help us.

No doubt you have heard or sung that magnificent section
of Handel's *Messiah* which uses the text of Isaiah 53:4–5:
"Surely he hath borne our griefs, and carried our sorrows.
. . . The chastisement of our peace was upon him." The enormousness of that passage never fails to overwhelm me,
whether I hear it sung or read aloud. That *is* good news, my
friend! Christ has redeemed—made whole—*all* our brokenness through taking every sin of ours unto himself.

No, young person, you have *not* blown it beyond redemp-
tion. Yes, grieving friend, there is indeed vitality in life beyond your loss. And yes, defeated worker, you indeed have
value and can be supportive to another downcast soul. Genu-
inely understand that "new life in Christ" means allowing
him to carry our griefs and sorrows and thus being in unity
with him. You—though wounded—can then have, through
Christ, God's perspective on the shattering events that have
happened to you. That is different from a saccharine, sen-
timental fatalism. It is the confidence that comes from claim-
ing with assurance, as did Paul, "We know that in everything
God works for good" (Rom. 8:28). You can take the next
step, do the next thing, with your brokenness redeemed and
made whole.

> He gives vigour to the weary,
> new strength to the exhausted.
> Young men may grow weary and faint,
> even in their prime they may stumble and fall;
> but those who look to the LORD will win new
>   strength,
> they will grow wings like eagles;
> they will run and not be weary,
> they will march on and never grow faint.
>   (Isa. 40:29–31, NEB)

This has been the faith of millions for centuries. It was the conviction of Dietrich Bonhoeffer, the Lutheran pastor and theologian who was arrested by the Gestapo in Germany and charged with conspiring with others to kill Hitler. In April of 1945, he held a service for the prisoners where he was confined. When he finished his last prayer, two officers entered the room and ordered Bonhoeffer to come with them. He and his fellow prisoners knew that this meant for him a hanging on the scaffold, so they bade him good-by. He drew aside the man who was later to become his biographer, Eberhard Bethge, and said in a low voice, "This is the end. For me the beginning of life" (Dietrich Bonhoeffer, *Letters and Papers from Prison,* p. 11; London: SCM Press, 1968).

Wholeness: Health and Salvation

The first translation of the whole Bible into English, made in the fourteenth century by John Wycliffe and others, renders the word for salvation as "health." Health is a state of body and mind in which all parts are performing in harmony. That kind of harmonious functioning is wholeness, fitting correctly into the pattern of God's design or purpose for each of us in the world, as set forth in Ephesians 1:10, "to unite all things in him." In spite of our brokenness, Christ has come to liberate us, "to let the broken victims go free" (Luke 4:18). In him all things are made new, not *un*broken. Rather, although they have been broken and shattered, in Christ all things are restored to wholeness. That is your hope and mine, and our salvation in which we rejoice.

Questions for Thought and Discussion

Chapter 1. Bondage

1. How is your own freedom limited by others? by events?
2. List the bondages of which you would like to be free.

Chapter 2: Loneliness

Can you think of creative uses of loneliness other than those dealt with in this chapter?

Chapter 3: Boredom

1. Describe methods you use to battle boredom.
2. Why will boredom become a major issue in America's technological society?

Chapter 4: Anxiety

1. Distinguish between anxiety and fear.
2. Is Jesus' remedy for anxiety too idealistic for today?

Chapter 5: Distrust

1. State the difference between being trusting and being gullible.

2. How can you build trust in public institutions at a time when trust is being eroded away?

Chapter 6: Despair

1. Suggest steps that you can take to dispel a sense of hopelessness.

2. Why do some people appear to come through crises with such ease?

Bibliography

Chapter 1: Bondage

Brooks, D. P. *Free to Be Christian.* Broadman Press, 1981.

Brown, Delwin. *To Set at Liberty: Christian Faith and Human Freedom.* Orbis Books, 1981.

Ellul, Jacques. *The Ethics of Freedom.* Tr. and ed. by Geoffrey W. Bromiley. Wm. B. Eerdmans Publishing Co., 1976.

Chapter 2: Loneliness

Hartog, Joseph, et al. (eds.). *The Anatomy of Loneliness.* International Universities Press, 1980.

Lynch, James J. *The Broken Heart: The Medical Consequences of Loneliness.* Basic Books, 1977.

Moustakas, Clark E. *The Touch of Loneliness.* Prentice-Hall, 1975.

Tournier, Paul. *Escape from Loneliness.* Tr. by J. S. Gilmour. Westminster Press, 1976.

Chapter 3: Boredom

Keen, Sam. *What to Do When You're Bored and Blue.* Wideview Books, Putnam Publishing Group, 1981.

Nisbet, Robert. "Boredom," in Robert Nisbet, *Prejudices: A*

Philosophical Dictionary. Harvard University Press, 1982.

Smith, Richard. "Boredom: A Review," *Human Factors,* Vol. 23, No. 3 (1981), pp. 329–340.

Chapter 4: Anxiety

Kierkegaard, Søren. *The Concept of Anxiety.* Ed. and tr. by Reidar Thomte. Princeton University Press, 1980.

May, Rollo. *The Meaning of Anxiety.* Rev. ed. W. W. Norton & Co., 1977.

Oates, Wayne. *Anxiety in Christian Experience.* Westminster Press, 1955.

Tillich, Paul. *The Courage to Be.* Yale University Press, 1952.

Chapter 5: Distrust

Bok, Sissela. *Lying: Moral Choice in Public and Private Life.* Pantheon Books, Random House, 1978, Chapter 2.

Rotter, Julian B. "Trust and Gullibility," *Psychology Today,* Oct. 1980, pp. 35–42, 102.

Shaver, Phillip. "The Public Trust," *Psychology Today,* Oct. 1980, pp. 45–49, 102.

Chapter 6: Despair

Boisen, Anton. *Out of the Depths.* Harper & Brothers, 1960.

Fosdick, Harry Emerson. *The Living of These Days.* Harper & Brothers, 1956.

Oates, Wayne. *Life's Detours.* Nashville: The Upper Room, 1974.

––––––. *The Struggle to Be Free: My Story and Your Story.* Westminster Press, 1983.

Notes